TOUCH
IN EARLY
DEVELOPMENT

TOUCH
IN EARLY
DEVELOPMENT

Edited by

TIFFANY M. FIELD
University of Miami School of Medicine

LEA
LAWRENCE ERLBAUM ASSOCIATES, PUBLISHERS
1995   Mahwah, New Jersey   Hove, UK

Lawrence Erlbaum Associates, Inc., Publishers
10 Industrial Avenue
Mahwah, New Jersey 07470

Library of Congress Cataloging-in-Publication Data
Touch in early development / edited by Tiffany M. Field.
   p.   cm.
  Includes indexes.
  ISBN 0-8058-1890-1
  1. Infants—Development—Congresses. 2. Touch in infants—
Congresses. 3. Touch—Therapeutic use—Congresses. I. Field, Tiffany.
RJ134.T68 1995
612.8'8—dc20
                                          95-12173
                                           CIP

Printed in the United States of America
10 9 8 7 6 5 4 3 2 1

Contents

Preface

Touch in Infancy was the title of a symposium held to celebrate the opening of the Touch Research Institute (TRI), the first of its kind in the world. There were already institutes for all the other senses, but, even though touch is the largest sense organ in the body, it is the one that has been the most neglected. The TRI is designed to conduct basic research on touch and on the skin, and to work with wellness programs, such as massage therapy and other kinds of touch therapies, to facilitate better health and to treat various diseases. It is located at the University of Miami School of Medicine and has been partially supported by very generous funding from the Johnson & Johnson Company and by grants from the National Institutes of Health. Those monies have enabled us to establish this multifaculty, multidiscipline, multiuniversity institute.

The opening symposium of the TRI was dedicated to Bob Rock, who was one of the initial founders of the institute and whose great ideas, unfortunately, came to fruition a few weeks after his untimely death. The institute and the symposium are a tribute to him.

The presentations made at the institute's opening are published in this volume. Snippets from those presentations are included in this preface. The first section of this volume highlights the importance of touch for the growth and development of the fetus, the newborn, and the growing infant. The volume begins with a chapter by Ashley Montagu, who speaks to the significance of touch for our species across all ages. Berry Brazelton then writes about touch and the fetus and the need for an assessment of the fetus. In a chapter on the need for touch during labor and delivery, Marshall Klaus introduces the *doula*, someone who comforts the laboring mother with touch. Gene Anderson's chapter focuses on the critical role of touch for the premature infant's development, introducing the kangaroo care method. Moving into infancy, Ed Tronick talks about the compensatory role of touch stimulation for infants who have unresponsive (e.g., depressed) parents. In a developmental trajectory starting from the prenatal period and ending in infancy, these authors highlight the critical role that touch plays in growth and development.

Ashley Montagu

Ashley Montagu is a world renowned anthropologist and the author of many books, including *Touching*, which has sold over a half million copies, and *The Natural Superiority of Women*. In his chapter on touch, he highlights and connects work from these two volumes. Montagu's basic thesis is that touch is adaptive in evolution as a form of social communication that crosses species, cultures, genders, and age groups. He offers several examples of touch deprivation: Without touch, there may be growth deprivation, communication failures, aggression, and war. It is perplexing in this light that touch has been the most neglected sense.

Dr. Montagu uses humor to criticize the experts from other times, and it can also be applied to the experts of current times who are advocating and mandating minimal touch (e.g., for the intensive care of neonates) or no touch (e.g., for nursery school children). Attitudes have not changed, unfortunately. We just do not touch for different reasons. In earlier years, experts were worried we would spoil the child, and today experts are worried that children could be abused if teachers were allowed to touch them. On one side of the world, Romanian orphans are attaining half their expected height because of touch deprivation, and on the other side, American teachers are not allowed to touch children for fear of child abuse accusations. The stories are very much the same as those in England reported by Ashley Montagu. The stories he tells frame a context in which the data reported in later chapters must be taken very seriously.

T. Berry Brazelton

Berry Brazelton is the co-author, with me, of *Advances in Touch*, based on a round table sponsored by Johnson & Johnson.

Dr. Brazelton developed the world's most widely used neonatal assessment scale, the Brazelton Neonatal Behavior Assessment Scale; its importance cannot be overrated. It has made both professionals and parents more aware of the amazing skills of the newborn and the importance of nurturing these skills from the time of birth.

Dr. Brazelton is now turning his attention to fetal assessment. A fetal assessment scale could be instrumental in detecting risk conditions in utero calling for pregnancy interventions, but it would also be useful for learning more about fetal development and, particularly, about how touch (the primary source of stimulation for the fetus) is perceived by the fetus and enhances prenatal learning. In a sense, tactile stimulation not only stimulates the growth of the fetus, but is the primary source of communication with the fetus (i.e., sound vibrations and amniotic fluid movements).

Marshall Klaus

Marshall Klaus and his wife have written a book called *The Amazing Newborn*; he also produced a film by the same name. Marshall has coined many useful terms for us, including *lying-in* and *rooming-in*, having established one of the first such arrangements in an obstetric hospital. He also coined the terms *bonding* and *doula*.

Dr. Klaus demonstrates the power of touch in labor and delivery. As we know from data on doula-assisted deliveries and data from mothers massaged during labor and delivery, touch significantly reduces anxiety in pregnant women. The reduction in psychological anxiety and its physiological manifestations (cortisol levels) contributes to a better (less stressed) prenatal environment for the fetus.

Gene Anderson

Gene Anderson has been instrumental in fostering many kinds of touch stimulation for preterm infants. First, she promoted stimulation of the intraoral cavity (the mouth) by having babies suck on pacifiers. In a collaborative study with her, my colleagues and I found that preemies sucking on pacifiers during tube-feedings were able to graduate to bottle-feeding several days earlier, were easier to feed, gained more weight, and were discharged from the hospital several days earlier than controls (resulting in significant cost savings). She is now suggesting that *kangaroo care*, tactile stimulation over much larger body surfaces, can significantly improve the care of preterm newborns. Gene Anderson's remarks are basically continuous with those of Marshall Klaus and Berry Brazelton, advocating continuous tactile stimulation for the growth and development of young organisms. It is hard to imagine human beings being kangaroos, but they actually like it very much.

Edward Z. Tronick

Recently Edward Tronick and others have been using touch to reduce the stress infants show when they encounter stressful situations, such as an unresponsive person. Dr. Tronick's message is that depressed mothers or very busy mothers, such as the Efe pygmy, can compensate for their infants' stress by providing extra touch. In the case of the pygmy mothers, the child is passed around to several caregiving adults and children. In the case of depressed mothers who are not very stimulating with their faces or voices, tactile stimulation can be added.

His chapter also explores the intriguing idea that touch conveys specific messages.

The next section of the volume reviews animal model research that has focused on underlying mechanisms to explain the touch–growth and touch–development relationships noted in the research on human infants. Saul Schanberg, Michael Leon, and Steven Suomi have used deprivation models with rat pups and infant monkeys to determine physiological, biochemical, and immune effects of various forms of sensory deprivation, including touch deprivation. These have, in turn, informed the touch therapy intervention models used with human infants, which I review in the final chapter. This back and forth movement between animal and human models is critical for the advancement of the field.

Saul Schanberg

Dr. Schanberg has designed a model curriculum for medical schools involving touch. Touch therapy, which (before drug therapy) was the foundation of medicine, is now returning to medical school curricula.

He has also recently discovered a gene for the touch–growth relationship. Much of his work with animal models has laid the foundation for, or at least informed, the work on tactile stimulation of preterm infants.

Michael Leon

Dr. Leon, one of the world's most renowned neuroscientists, is, fortunately, studying touch. In his research, he has noted that rats can come to prefer odors not previously preferred simply because the odors are accompanied by touch. He has also discovered that moderate levels of norepinephrine (but not low or high levels) seem to mediate touch effects so that a noradrenergic agonist, just like touch, when paired with a nonpreferred odor will develop into a preference. That is a very interesting finding because in some tactile stimulation studies norepinephrine increases and in others it decreases. It could be that tactile stimulation helps adjust norepinephrine levels to an optimal level. As with many functions, an inverted U-curve describes the relation between dose level and outcome. The other interesting aspect of this work is the intimate connection between the senses, in this case smell and touch, that appears to be present at least from birth.

Stephen Suomi

Steve Suomi is renowned for his pioneering work in the field of psychoneuroimmunology, using the monkey as a model. His data suggest that touch has significant critical effects on the immune system. It is interesting and troublesome that Harry Harlow's pioneering work of 30 years ago with monkeys is only now being applied to humans. Like its positive effects on the immune system in monkeys, the Touch Research Institute has just documented the positive effects of massage therapy on the immune systems of HIV men. Following a month of massage therapy, the number of their natural killer cells increased.

Tiffany Field

The effects of massage therapy on infants are elaborated in this chapter. For any research to get adopted into practice some understanding of the underlying physiological/biochemical mechanism is necessary. The convergence of animal and human research and basic and applied research help this process move along at a faster rate.

ACKNOWLEDGMENT

Jim Burke had the vision that was basically responsible for the founding of the Touch Research Institute. A few years ago, when he was the chief executive officer of Johnson & Johnson, before he became the president of "A Partnership for a Drug Free America," he conducted a press conference, this excerpt of which conveys the message of this volume:

> I think we will develop models suggesting that we can enhance the immune system by touch. I have no doubt that people who are well loved from birth to death have less disease; I would bet everything I own on that. Regardless of what genetic input has impacted our lives, I just have to believe that what life is all about is learning to love each other. In that case, there has to be a positive outcome as it relates to illness. Illness is an abnormal state. Keep reminding yourself that the normal state is wellness; illness is abnormal. The normal person should be born and live 90 to 100 years (or wherever that clock stops) and then die. Anything in between should be viewed conceptually as an aberration, and if it is an aberration, then there is a way to prevent it from happening. If there is a way to prevent it from happening, we ought to be part of that process (if, in fact, we are one of the most notable health care companies in the world). That is the way to define *health*: the absence of disease. I think the prevention of disease will happen through touch. I think you are going to be able to find ways to prove that in animal and human models. Unfortunately, there are a lot of people in our society, for example, children, who are emotionally deprived, deprived of touch, and I think you are going to find that there are whole sets of diseases that come from touch deprivation.

Jim Burke had that vision. Only a few years since he talked about altering the immune system, we now have data suggesting that touch, indeed, alters the immune system.

Tiffany M. Field

TOUCH
IN EARLY
DEVELOPMENT

Animadversions on the Development of a Theory of Touch

Ashley Montagu
Princeton, New Jersey

It is of great interest to me how ideas get started. One of the most amazing things to me, as I look back on my own history in connection with the development of ideas relating to the importance of touching, is that they originated in my childhood. I was born in England, a land full of people who, in a well-bred family at least, seldom touched each other, in which you apologized to your parents or siblings whenever you touched them accidentally. This, of course, was the rule in well-bred families, so-called because they regularly devoted more care to breeding horses than caring for children. In the uppermost classes, the custom was that you married a horse from your own stable. The couple would then occupy separate rooms in remote wings of the house. They very rarely met because, most of the time, the husband was out hunting, fishing, and shooting or traveling abroad. So, in the ruling classes, the class that set the pattern for all others, very little touching occurred. At an early age, boys were sent away to public school—so called because the public was not admitted to it. In most English families, there was very little, if any, touching, and very little love. When I was small, the usual approach to me by a male adult visitor to our household, was to muss up my hair, tweak my cheek, sometimes flick my ear, and then announce, "What a nice boy you are," and, with easy indifference, to depart—leaving me with the puzzling problem of resolving how one can be a nice boy, and at the same time be so hurt and humiliated. So, I began to wonder about adult males. What impressed me deeply is that women never behaved in anything approaching so unpleasant a manner. Women were really interested in you as a human being, and would pat you on the head or the cheek or under the chin, and always behaved like caring civilized human beings who were genuinely interested in you.

That was the origin, I suspect, of my book, *The Natural Superiority of Women* (Montagu, 1953). Why were men and women so different? Could men ever have been children? From their conduct, it seemed to me that they never could have been, for from their behavior they clearly didn't understand children. I concluded that men were created adults from the very beginning. The fact is that most Englishmen of my generation never were children. As children, they had lived in a territory occupied by enemies—adults, parents and other socializers, tyrants—who ordered them about with scarcely an explanation. This was the beginning of my interest in how human beings become what they become.

At a very early age, I decided I would become what was called as late as the third decade of the 20th century, an *alienist*, someone who studied and treated those who were mentally deranged, or alienated from themselves or the world in which they were living, what we now call a *psychiatrist*. At my first dinner at a freshmen welcome, I was seated next to a student from the Middle East who asked me what I was proposing to be. I replied, "An alienist." I had to explain to him what an alienist did, because his English was not what it might have been. There was then a long pause. When suddenly the dawn broke on him, he exclaimed, "Ah, a doctor of fools." His English may not have been formally sound, but there was no doubt that he had figured out that it had something to do with the study of the id by the odd.

At college, I had the good fortune to meet three professors, one who professed psychoanalytic psychology, another who was a mathematically inclined cognitive psychologist, and a third, who professed anatomy, but was devoted to anthropology: J. C. Flügel, Charles Spearman, and Elliot Smith, respectively. Spearman set up a special meeting with Elliot Smith, at which they gently quizzed me. They decided that I could roam around freely and not have to worry too much about examinations. Needless to say, I was very lucky and took every course that interested me. The result was a very unusual education, which has enabled me to perceive relationships between things that others have not seen as easily. We don't have anything resembling education in the Western world. What passes for such is mostly instruction, a very different thing. The origin of the word *education* is the Latin, *educare* (or, to anglicize, *edu-care*). This is very good because the word *care*, as you probably know, in spite of the King James translation of the Latin word *caritas*, means "love," and not "charity," as it was inaccurately translated; it means "to care for." When you talk about a caregiver, you really should mean "one who loves the other." Insofar as touch is concerned, as a result of my lifelong studies in these areas, I know very clearly as a scientist that love and touching are two faces of the same thing. For example, I am a passionate dancer, in the style of Fred Astaire, but not within light-years of his elegance and skill. When we have concluded dancing, I may say to my partner, "Do you know what this is? It is a declaration of love." That sometimes results in an incomprehensible stare, but generally it is quickly understood, for what it is: the beginning of a deep friendship. So, the recognition of the relationship between love and caring and touching came to me in a series of gradual steps, which I can not possibly explicate in so little space.

Following a stint at the British Museum (Natural History) and another as curator of physical anthropology at the Wellcome Historical Medical Museum in London, I was an assistant professor of anatomy in the Graduate School of Medicine at New York University. It was my lot to be in charge of the dissecting room, which was a wonderful experience, because I had 100 students for 3 hours every morning, 5 days a week. A lot of investigation and experimentation could go on during that time, not only *with* but also *of* the students, as well as with and of the instructors who were assisting in the dissecting room. A considerable amount of research and publication started in that laboratory. What was most unfortunate was the experience of seeing that many of the students who arrived with some interest in the humanity of human beings left with scarcely any interest in human beings at all. The trade school put an end to all that. As they passed through, they went through the process of dehumanization: the loss of understanding of what medicine should be, the loss of sensitivity and caring. With most of their training devoted to tests and disease, and hardly any to its prevention, and the maintenance of health, there was literally nothing taught relating to the human being. Because I was at N.Y.U. as an anthropologist and anatomist, my interests embraced every department, and I took advantage of the opportunities for observation and research they willingly offered, including those of Bellevue: obstetrics, pediatrics, radiology, genetics, and even teaching and doing research in the dental school. All of this led to a greater understanding of the interrelatedness of these branches of knowledge, and a good deal else. It was all very exciting and illuminating, and I felt very grateful.

Apropos of this, for many years I have longed to give a lecture entitled "Radiology and Love." I *have* given the lecture, but no medical school would permit me to use that title because my kind sponsors said, "No one will understand what on earth you are talking about from that title. What does radiology have to do with love?" Radiology has a great deal to do with love, and affords a powerful means of showing what a fundamental role love, or its absence, can play in the physiological developmental history of a person. If, for example, during a period of growth the organism has suffered a lack of love, you will see bilaterally transverse lines of retarded growth at the distal ends of the tibia and radius of the individual (Dixon & Sarnat, 1985). You will also often see such lines (sometimes called "Harris lines") in the x-ray of metacarpal bones of a newborn baby if the mother has had an emotionally disturbing pregnancy. All seven, or most, of the carpal bones may show radio-opaque lines toward the periphery of the bones. At the lower end of the tibia, there may be as many as 12 of these lines of retarded growth of varying thickness, depending on the frequency and duration during which the individual has been either bedridden or unloved during development. These show up very clearly in animals also. I don't recall how or when I first learned about these lines of retarded growth, but it was long before I came across *Bone Growth in Health and Disease*, whose author, H. A. Harris (1933), happened to be a lecturer in the department of anatomy when I was a student in the early 1920s at University College. Harris's book has been out of print for many years. I tried to persuade the publisher to reprint it, unsuccessfully, alas. Some day, it should be republished.

When I was at N.Y.U., I became very interested in the whole process of obstetrics and the mother–child relationship. At the time, breast-feeding had been largely replaced by bottle-feeding. This was because in the 1930s, 1940s, and 1950s, both the mothers and the nurses had been brought up on the widely influential opinions of Luther Emmett Holt, professor of pediatrics at Cornell University Medical School, the most influential pediatrician of his day. In 1894, Holt published a booklet entitled *The Care and Feeding of Children*; the 15th and last edition appeared 40 years later, and it continued to be printed by the U.S. Printing Office and distributed freely by the government to millions of mothers (Holt, 1935). In this booklet, Holt recommended bottle-feeding as being just as good as breast-feeding, and strongly recommended the abolition of the cradle, while giving such sage advice as never to pick up a child, no matter how long it cries, and of course to feed it only at 4-hour intervals. In the early 1920s, the evaluator of contemporary trail blazers, Grant Overton, wrote of Holt's book that it represented "possibly the greatest service to humanity in our time" (Overton, 1924, p. 117).

Another great influence was the founder of behaviorism, John Broadus Watson, head of the department of psychology at Johns Hopkins University (Cohen, 1979). In 1928, he published *The Psychological Care of Infant and Child* (Watson, 1928). The book opened with a poem in tribute to Holt's book and its influence. Bertrand Russell, the distinguished mathematician and philosopher recommended the book effusively. *The Atlantic Monthly* reviewed it as a book that should be read by everyone, while *Parents Magazine* said it should be on every mother's bookshelf. So much, then, for the opinions of the "authorities." Here is Professor Watson, in his own words: "Nearly all of us have suffered from over-coddling. How does it show? It shows as *invalidism*. As adults we have too many aches and pains" (pp. 75–76). "Over-conditioning in love is the rule" (p. 78). "Kissing the youngster on the forehead, on the back of the hand, patting it on the head once in a while, would be all the petting needed for a baby to learn that it is growing up in a kindly home" (p. 81). "There is a sensible way of treating children. Treat them as though they were young adults. Dress them with care and circumspection. Let your behavior always be objective and kindly firm. Never hug and kiss them, never let them sit in your lap. If you must, kiss them once on the forehead when they say goodnight. Shake hands with them, in the morning" (pp. 81–82). "No child should get commendation and notice and petting every time it does something it ought to be doing anyway" (p. 84). And so Watson went perniciously on.

Who can calculate the human damage that these "authorities" did? It was undoubtedly considerable. The model and the basic pattern on which all human behavior should be based is that which is set at the moment of the appearance of a human being on this earth, namely, the loving behavior shared between a loving mother and her child, the reciprocity of love and its growth. Babies are born with the need for love, not only to be loved, but also to love others, to grow to love others *more* than they love themselves. It is important to love others more than you love yourself, as, indeed, a mother loves her child. It is the love between mother and child that is the basic pattern of the loving connectedness that we are designed by our very nature to follow and to grow in all the days of our lives.

We are aware of the existence of the basic physical needs that must be satisfied if we are to survive: oxygen, food, liquid, activity, rest, sleep, bowel and bladder elimination, and the avoidance of noxious stimuli. We cannot ignore the need for love and touching.

One of the most wonderful courses I took as a student was my 2-year course on linguistics with Franz Boas at Columbia University in 1934–1936. We studied the grammar of five American Indian languages: Algonquin, Teton Dakotan, Siouan, Kwakiutal, and Iroquoian. One of my great discoveries during this experience was that we become more enamored of the myths that are enshrined in our words than we are in the truths that they obscure. So, in the discovery of the meaning of words one may find the meaning of what one learns at one's mother's breast. As the psalmist wrote, "I will lift up mine eyes unto the hills, whence cometh my help" (Psalm 121).

Speaking of mother's breast, take the example of breast-feeding. Breast-feeding has been observed for many, many years, millions of times, but what really happens at the breast? We say that the baby *sucks* at the breast, but that is wrong. He or she would not get enough of the elements necessary for survival that way. What the baby does is to *suckle*, that is, to turn its mouth into an hermetically sealed suction pump. In each cheek, there is a ball of fat almost the size of a golf ball; this gives the baby its rounded cheeks. On each side of the inner cheek there is a membrane (the gingival membrane) that attaches the cheek to the gum, all in readiness for the baby to apply its lips and gums to the areola region. Thus, the nipple rests between the upper and lower gums and the hard palate and the baby's tongue, and the tongue plays an active role in compressing the nipple against the hard palate.

So, we see that words often mislead and create errors that their continued usage perpetuates. Definitions cannot be meaningful at the beginning of an inquiry: they can only be so at the end of one. We should be learning how to use words as if they were experiments that we are observing. When, for example, we use a word such as *observation*, it must be used as an act of experiment, experimenting in one's mind as we are thinking. Thinking is problem solving, and it is pleasurable hard work. It is not simple stereotyping or a cliché. In observation, one should be critically examining what one is observing, weighing, analyzing—in short, being critical, in the Greek sense of the word *Kritikos*, doing the best with one's mind, being careful not to add ambiguity of words to confusion of thought. What you *do* is what you believe, not what you *think* you believe.

There is a trenchant quatrain that puts the point beautifully. It was written by Jane Taylor, who lived at the beginning of the 19th century:

> Man, a thinking being is defined,
> But few use the grand prerogative of mind,
> How few think well of the thinking few,
> How many never think who think they do.

In conclusion, let me give a brief account of the origin of *Touching* (Montagu, 1986). In November 1944, while teaching anatomy in medical school, I was invited by the Sociology Department (later the Department of Social Relations) at Harvard, to give one course on the socialization of the child, another on "race," and a seminar together with Talcott Parsons, on American culture. In preparation for the first course I set to organizing the material I had been gathering for many years on the nature of human development. During the course of my survey of the literature in the early 1940s, I had read an article on the thyroid gland, published in 1922, by the anatomist Frederick S. Hammet of the Wistar Institute in Philadelphia, which showed that parathyroidectomized rats that had been "gentled" were far better operative risks than those that had not (Hammet, 1921, 1922). When I read this article, fireworks went off in my head. It was gentling that had made the difference! Hammet, in spite of some speculation, had, unfortunately, missed the significance of tactile stimulation as a basic need for probably all mammals. Immediately things began to click in my mind. One after another, many articles I had read on physiological and behavioral development, like so any pieces in a puzzle, began to fall into place. Maternal deprivation in animals and humans, isolation, licking of the young in animals, breast-feeding, the species trait of touching in primates, and much else, all came to heuristic support for the theory that tactual stimulation was a fundamental factor in the healthy development of organisms (Park & Mason, 1957). The many relevant works I had read are all discussed in *The Direction of Human Development* (Montagu, 1955), and in *Touching* (Montagu, 1971). I cannot list them all here, but the workers who contributed most to the development of my ideas were René Spitz (1945), Lester Sontag (1938), William Goldfarb (1943), James Robertson (1958), Henry Chapin (1915), J. Brennemann (1932), and Fritz Talbot (1941).

There was also Old Anna. Before World War I, Dr. Fritz Talbot of Boston was escorted through the Children's Hospital in Dusseldorf by the Director, Dr. Arthur Schlossmann. The wards were very neat and tidy, but Dr. Talbot's curiosity was piqued by the sight of a squat old lady waddling ahead of them down the corridor, carrying a baby on her hip. "Who's that?" inquired Dr. Talbot. "Oh," said Dr. Schlossmann, "that is Old Anna. When we have done everything medically we can for a baby, and it is still not doing well, we turn it over to Old Anna, and she is always successful in restoring it to vigor."

When Dr. Talbot returned to his duties in Boston he instructed the nurses and interns on his wards to pick up and hold the babies. The ensuing improvement in the welfare of the babies would have gratified Old Anna. It is not often that the Old Annas of this world have been appreciated. It gives me special pleasure to think of her and how much we owe her.

Pulling together all the evidence derived from these and other sources gave me the sort of feeling that John Keats must have experienced when he first read George Chapman's English translation of Homer, which he celebrated in his beautiful sonnet, "On First Looking Into Chapman's Homer":

> Much have I travell'd in the realms of gold
> And many goodly states and kingdoms seen;
> Round many western islands have I been
> Which bards in fealty to Apollo hold.
> Oft of one wide expanse had I been told
> That deep-brow'd Homer ruled as his demesne;

Yet never did I breathe its pure serene
Till I heard Chapman speak out loud and bold:
Then felt I like some watcher of the skies
When a new planet swims into his ken;
Or like stout Cortez, when with eagle eyes
He stared at the Pacific—and all his men
Look'd at each other with a wild surmise—
Silent, upon a peak in Darien.

I had come upon Touching. The rest is history.

Ashley Montagu—Question and Answer Session

QUESTION: When you refer to what lack of love does to the bones are you referring to "Harris Lines"?

ANSWER: Yes.

QUESTION: Because that is an effect of various kinds of stress?

ANSWER: Yes, any kind of stress during the growing period. Stress is what produces shock and this is a very important subject. In our culture the chief cause of stress is reality!

QUESTION: In regard to your comment that "education" is not the best way to go about getting educated, what is an alternative for someone 15, 20, or 25 years old who wants to be educated when he or she is faced with our educational system today?

ANSWER: Essentially, education is a process. The real meaning of the word *educare* as it was used by the Romans is "to nourish and to cause to grow." To nourish and to grow what? Our basic behavioral needs, as I call them. The most important of these needs is the need for love—not only to be loved, but the need also to love others. The basic behavioral needs are the need for speech, thinking, for sensitivity, for wonder, for explorativeness, for curiosity, for experimentalness, for imagination, for fantasy, for knowledge, for learning, for work, for creativity, for enthusiasm, for play, for dance, for song, and for touch. These needs constitute our in-built system of values, and what they require for development is the encouragement of love. It is the satisfaction of those needs which is the most important part of education. Hence, the process of re-education consists in encouraging these basic behavioral needs in ourselves, and in others, by acting them out, by demonstrative communication. We can all re-educate ourselves to become warm, loving, creative human beings, who, loving ourselves, love others more than ourselves. All else is secondary. And finally, to remember that an educated person is one who has overcome the deficiencies of the educational system.

REFERENCES

Brennemann, J. (1932). The infant ward. *American Journal of Diseases of Children, 43,* 577.

Chapin, H. (1915). A plea for accurate statistics in infants' institutions. *Transactions of the American Pediatric Society, 27.*

Cohen, J. D. (1979). *J. B. Watson, the founder of behaviorism: A biography.* Boston: Routledge & Kegan Paul.

Dixon, A. D., & Sarnat, B. G. (1985). *Normal and abnormal bone growth.* New York: Alan R. Liss.

Goldfarb, W. (1943). The effects of early institutional care on adolescent personality. *Journal of Experimental Education, 12,* 106–129.

Hammett, F. S. (1921). Studies of the thyroid apparatus: I. *American Journal of Physiology, 56,* 196–204.

Hammet, F. S. (1922). Studies of the thyroid apparatus: V. *Endocrinology, 6,* 221–229.

Harris, H. A. (1933). *Bone growth in health and disease.* London: Oxford University Press.

Holt, L. E. (1935). *The care and feeding of children.* New York: Appleton-Century. (Original work published 1894)

Montagu, A. (1986). *Touching: The human significance of the skin.* New York: Harper & Row.

Park, E. A., & Mason, H. H. (1957). *Pediatric profiles.* In B. S. Veeder (Ed.). St. Louis: Mosby.

Patton, R. G., & Gardner, L. I. (1963). *Growth failure in maternal deprivation.* Springfield, IL: Thomas.

Robertson, J. (1958). *Young children in hospital.* Tavistock: London.

Sontag, L. W. (1938). Evidences of disturbed prenatal and neonatal growth in bones of infants at one month. *American Journal of Diseases of Children, 53,* 1248–1255.

Spitz, R. (1945). Hospitalism. *The Psychoanalytic Study of the Child, 1,* 53–74.

Talbot, F. (1941). Discussion. *Transactions of the American Pediatric Society, 62,* 469.

Watson, J. B. (1928). *Psychological care of infant and child.* New York: Norton.

CHAPTER TWO

Fetal Observations: Could They Relate to Another Modality, Such as Touch?

T. Berry Brazelton, M.D.
Children's Hospital, Harvard Medical School

Thirty-five years ago, when my colleagues and I started to develop the neonatal assessment scale (Brazelton, 1973), the common belief was that babies could not see or hear at birth. I wondered how people could think that. Dr. Sally Provence would pick up a newborn baby and dance with the baby like a ballet dancer. The two of them would get into a synchrony that was astounding. The baby would come alive. When I went out to learn the Graham Scale (Graham, 1956) from Bette Caldwell, we had a baby who was not responsive visually. She said, "Oh, we have to get his energy up into his eyes to show you how he can follow this red ball." She gave the baby a pacifier. He began to suck. "Now, we have his energy up here." Then she gradually pulled out the pacifier so the baby gave up sucking. At the right moment, she took the pacifier out and placed the red wool ball in front of his eyes. His eyes opened up and he began to follow the bright ball of wool back and forth. I was no longer just talking about whether a baby could see and hear; I was observing that the whole organism responded visually and auditorially, using all its resources: state control, autonomic control, motor responses—all were a necessary part of this response.

This started me on the quest for what babies could not only see and hear, but what they would do in order to see and hear. This fit in with my work with parents and my wish to identify with them as they faced the job of helping a new baby to learn. What has become more and more apparent to me is that the work of attachment starts in pregnancy (Brazelton & Cramer, 1990) with the first indication of, "Oh, my God, I'm going to be a parent—how did I ever let myself in for this? Can I live up to it?" Of course, there is ambivalence. "Can I do it? Do I want to?" Ambivalence is a powerful force; no passion exists without ambivalence. Examples of the ambivalence that comes up at that point is, "Will I ever get to be a parent, what kind of a parent will I be? Will I have to be like my parents?" Because most of my practice now is grandchildren, I can pull out the parents' old records and say, "Tell me what you remember about being a baby or a child, because I have all of your records right here and we can compare notes." They remind me of what they remember from childhood, and I can remind them of what I remember from my records.

The marvelous thing is that when they start off with their own new babies, they all say the same thing, "I don't want to be like my parent. Do you remember what she was like?" I say, "Well, yes, I do, and I will help you do it your way." But when they hit a snag, for example, the irritable crying at the end of the day in the first few weeks, new parents invariably do the same things their parents did. This repetition seems to be inevitable.

Parents always want to share their fantasies about the baby-to-be. All parents dream of two babies, the perfect three-month-old that you pick up and ask, "How are you doing?" and the baby says, "Ooh," and you say, "That's right, now come on, give us one more," and the baby says, "Ooh," a second and third time. This dream baby responds to all of your elicitations. This is the kind of perfect three-month-old everybody dreams of. Then there is the imperfect baby to balance that, the damaged infant all parents dream of. They worry about whether they'll have a damaged baby and how they'll ever parent it. The baby is calling up a kind of alarm reaction, so the parents can be ready to identify with whatever kind of baby they get. These two babies are balanced in the dreams and fantasies of new parents as they ready themselves for the baby they will encounter (Brazelton & Cramer, 1990).

Parents also try to understand the real fetus, and they work hard at it. One of my goals is to understand this fetus. Another goal is to identify the intrauterine effects of the different variables that we can identify, such as malnutrition, exposure to alcohol and drugs. We need to be able to identify a stressed fetus before delivery. We need an assessment of fetal behavior so that we can have a way of predicting the outcome of the newborn at delivery and be ready for necessary supports.

One of my West Coast colleagues made a film of a mother taking a dose of crack at twenty weeks of gestation. The mother gave us permission to film the baby, but she has not yet given us permission to circulate the film. I would like to circulate it to the high schools around the country. As we were filming the fetus by ultrasound, the mother said, "Don't ask me to give up my habit. I would rather give up my fetus." She took a dose of crack; eighteen seconds later, the drug crossed the placenta. The baby started to flip over and over. He flipped relentlessly for 2½ hours. The heart rate and motor activity became desynchronized. The mother's "high" came down within 25 minutes. One could see the pain increase in her face over time as she watched her baby's frantic activity. Finally, after 1½ hours, she said, "I can't stand this, I have to get into treatment." I'm happy to report that she did get into treatment. Maybe we could use this effect on the mother of watching her baby to influence her fetus's response. I would like to use ultrasound to capture the behavior of the fetus for women and men in pregnancy.

There also is evidence that a baby's outcome might be improved if we could induce labor at an optimal point to provide an environment outside the uterus when the fetus is being stressed in utero. We might be able to give it a better chance to recover under controlled situations. That led me to an interest in fetal behavior.

The other thread that led me to my interest was Lester Sontag's monitoring of fetuses in the 1950s (Sontag, Steele, & Lewis, 1969). He used a fetal monitor to assess the fetus's reaction as it was subjected to three different stimuli. He had the mother smoke a cigarette, he presented a loud noise, and then he introduced an emotional stimulus to the mother, such as the statement, "Your husband was just in an accident on the freeway." During these presentations, the baby's heart rate sped up, slowed down, and came to rest, in a homeostatic curve. Next, he took chronically stressed mothers, mothers with lots of kids, mothers who were chronic smokers, and mothers who had experienced traumatic events repeatedly, and presented their fetuses with the same three stimuli. These babies' heart rates also sped up, slowed down, and came to rest, but in a foreshortened curve. This intrigued me in terms of representing a learning model of learning to cope with intrauterine stress. This fits with some of the work done by Peter Nathanielsz on intrauterine movement (Nathanielsz, 1992). He has shown that babies who are slowed down in their behavior in the uterus do not contribute enough motor activity to the uterus during delivery, so the delivery becomes predictably longer. Dystocia and even hypoxia may accompany the delivery. The question that Milani-Comparetti and Gidoni (1967) raised was, "Are we already assuming that a vulnerable fetus comes into the delivery?" (p. 635). If it's a normal delivery, there is no problem, but if the dystocia leads to hypoxia and other stress, because he is already vulnerable, he can be more damaged by such insults. When we see a baby with cerebral palsy, we wonder whether the first nine months contributed to that vulnerability. This led to my interest in the intrauterine Neonatal Behavioral Assessment Scale (NBAS).

We shaped the fetal scale on the concept of states, as I did with the NBAS. There are four states of consciousness that a mother can identify in her fetus. If I ask a mother to keep a curve of the occurrence of these states over a 24-hour period, she will come up with a chart that looks very close to a cycling of them, day and night. Could we monitor them in a more precise way? State 1 is deep sleep, in which the fetus is essentially quiet and unresponsive. If it moves at all, it is with one or two jerks. It is not responsive to stimuli around the mother. Geoffrey Dawes alerted me to state 2 from his work with externalized fetal lambs. This state is accompanied by hiccups or jerky, repeated movements. If there is movement, it is a bit more organized. In this state, the baby might be a bit more alert to external stimuli. State 3 is that of activity: climbing the uterine wall. Not only do all parents, mothers and fathers, know when that is going to occur, but they know how to manipulate it. If the parents go out at night, it can be postponed by a half hour. Ultimately, the parents could be a source of monitoring, understanding the cycling of states. State 4 is the most exciting, an alert quiet state.

We can identify these states behaviorally if we watch for as much as three or four minutes; babies may then cycle out of them, depending on external stimuli. We have been trying to find out how much can be visualized within these states. There is evidence that a baby with cardiac nonvariability or repeated respiratory or jerky activity is already in trouble. We wonder whether motor control, which is so magnificently restricted by the uterus, could be monitored in a way that would show us the fetus's own attempts to keep its motor activity under control and differentiate that from pathological inactivity.

We have been using auditory and visual stimuli. We use a loud buzzer sounded eighteen inches from the abdomen. Vibration seems to be the most intrusive stimulus for the fetus, but this one is auditory, too. The first buzzer causes a massive startle of the whole uterus, the second buzzer causes less startle, and the third buzzer causes very little startle. By the fourth and fifth buzzer, there is no gross movement, but the fetus brings its hands up to its mouth and makes mouthing movements around its fist. As the hands come to the mouth, the fetus turns slightly away from the buzzer.

Next, we change stimuli. The uterus is said to be noisy, so you would think that the fetus would never hear a soft rattle; however, if you use a rattle from the NBAS, which is soft, and you rattle it right next to the abdomen, the fetus takes its hand away from its mouth, opens its eyes, and looks in the direction of the rattle.

If you stimulate with light, you first line up an operating room light in the line of vision about three feet away from the abdomen. With a flash of light, the fetus responds with a longer latency than with an auditory stimulus, but it finally startles. As you keep repeating the stimulation, the fetus habituates, stops moving, and turns its head away. Several fetuses have put their thumbs up to their mouths and closed their eyes. If we use a pinpoint light on the abdomen, the baby turns toward it and looks at it. What is so exciting is that the fetuses must maintain a state of attention and habituation in order to do this. They seem to have the capacity to control their own interfering motor activity. I have seen an inverse correlation in most of our work with the NBAS between interfering motor activity and the capacity to pay attention to prolonged stimulation. Here it is in the fetal stage.

We have identified certain elements as being important as predictors from many research projects using the Neonatal Behavioral Assessment Scale (NBAS). The ones which predict to optimal outcome in the neonate are: state control to both shut out and accept stimuli. State mastery seems to be the newborn's most important task. If we translate this to the fetus, variability, the capacity to master and pay attention and habituate can provide us with a way of measuring stress in the fetus that we can rely on to make a prenatal diagnosis of an overly stressed fetus.

My dream would be to combine modalities, including touch, to test fetal responsiveness. We know so much more than we used to. Touch is so powerful in the messages it sends. Think about the different messages we send with touch: learning how to prolong a state and how to transmit negative and positive stimuli. Couldn't we use those indirectly on the fetus? Of course, we would have to account for the mother's reaction, what kind of response it called up in her, not only on a conscious level but on a hormonal level. We would want to know the response of the fetus and the latency, and how it influences state controls. In this way, we could identify babies who were stressed and babies who were in an optimal condition for delivery.

**T. Berry Brazelton—
Question and Answer Session**

QUESTION: Do you think fetal activity is reflexive or organized?

ANSWER: I would hope it was something in between. I think there may be a reflexive element in it. However, I look for the kind of movement that is not just reflexive. Reflexive movement in the uterus is easy to pick out. As you get into the second state, and certainly in the third and fourth states, you find organized movement just as you do in the neonate, and that may take it out of the purely reflexive. A reflex may set it off, but then it gets organized. This movement may still occur at the midbrain level. The midbrain has important storage and learning that could go on at that level. I would hope that, just as we learned that the neonate has such incredible capacities, we have learned that we can begin to attribute organization to the fetus. It seems obvious to me that we take too simplistic a view toward genetic endowment of behavior, as if it wasn't already influenced in the uterus by experience. We have a study in Japan on the Goto Islands in which we look at Japanese neonates. This is a quiet little island where the mothers work hard all the time, but they don't lead the active, stressed lives of mothers in Tokyo. If you compare the neonates on the Goto Islands to the neonates in Tokyo and then to Japanese neonates in San Francisco, they're on a spectrum coming closer and closer to Caucasian. What you see in Japanese neonates at birth is that they have this beautiful delicate movement, like ballet dancers. Their fingers and toes are freed up and they are moving very quietly with practically no startle. Their alert state can be maintained for thirty minutes with a break, and they'll respond to a visual stimulus or a soft rattle; if it gets too loud, however, you lose them. If you value the relative hypersensitivity of their neonatal equipment and then combine that with the low-key movement for thirty minutes in the Gotos, when you go to Tokyo, it is already cut down significantly and the baby is more vigorous and has less prolonged attention. If you go to San Francisco, it is even more. In Caucasians, I can get three minutes without a break; however, if you get a Caucasian baby excited about a visual or auditory stimulus, it can get so intense that the baby throws off a startle or a Moro and you lose him. You would then have to bring him back and start all over again. I am not making guesses as to whether this is good or bad. I am saying that it needs to be respected as if the intrauterine effect of that genetic endowment is already operant. For example, if you watch mothers on the Goto Islands, you would see that they walk slowly up to the street sign, look slowly up and down the street, and then saunter across the street. If you go to Tokyo, you would see the mothers quickly walk up to the street sign, look quickly up and down, and quickly go across. Then if you go to San Francisco, you would see that the mothers quickly walk up to street and are watching their backs at the same time. These mothers' activity and tension must affect their fetuses. Isn't this a kind of incorporation of an effect on their genetic endowment? So, I would say that the kind of intrauterine expectancy that I would have for their behavior at birth as a reflection of genetic endowment would be significantly different across these conditions.

The Dubowitz Scale is useful here. It has two components. The external endowment features of the Dubowitz Scale follow a predictable map and correspond to the gestational age of the baby; however, if the other component, reflex behavior, is more than two points above the external endowment components, you should look for intrauterine stress. What happens is that reflex and motor behaviors speed up under stress, so that these babies are born relatively precocious in one area compared to the other. All of this comes down to the fact that babies adapt to their intrauterine conditions and "learn" from them.

QUESTION: Is the fetal scale available for use?

ANSWER: We are not near that, I fear. We don't have a normative base of subjects yet. I wish I could have shown you the video tape just to show you what we are seeing, so that you could say, "Crazy" or "Yes, it's there." I would also like to tease a couple of you into getting into the act and helping us do some definitive work. However, we are nowhere near there. It is going to take a lot of babies, and we have had only twelve so far.

ACKNOWLEDGMENTS

I would like to thank Eileen and Bob Rock, dear friends of ours for a long time, who have enriched our lives so much that I don't even like to think back on it, because it was so much fun. I would also like to thank Jim Dettre, Bonnie Petrauskus, and Steve Sawchuck, who kept the Johnson & Johnson Institute going long enough for J & J to get inspired enough to inspire Tiffany Field and Saul Schanberg to set up this wonderful Touch Research Institute. I look forward to the work of the Touch Research Institute because I think it will be able to identify just how powerful one modality can be. Of course, they have chosen the modality that is the most communicative and the most necessary to control the immature organism, so that it can pick up the messages we are offering and begin to incorporate them.

REFERENCES

Brazelton, T. B. (1973). *Neonatal Behavioral Assessment Scale*, National Spastics Foundation Monograph #88.

Brazelton, T. B., & Cramer, B. G. (1990). *The earliest relationship.* Reading, MA: Addison-Wesley.

Brazelton, T. B., Nugent, J. K., & Lester, B. M. (1987). Neonatal Behavioral Assessment Scale. In J. Osofsky (Ed.), *Handbook of infant development* (2nd ed., pp. 780–817). New York: Wiley.

Graham, F. K. (1956). Behavioral differences between normal and traumatized newborns in test procedures. *Psychological Monographs, 70.*

Milani-Comparetti, A., & Gidoni, E. (1967). Routine developmental examination in normal and retarded children. *Developmental Medicine and Child Neurology, 9,* 631–638.

Nathanielsz, P. W. (1992). *Life before birth and a time to be born.* Ithaca, NY: Promethean Press.

Sontag, L. W., Steele, W. G., & Lewis, M. (1969). The fetal and maternal response to environmental stress. *Human Development, 12,* 16–28.

CHAPTER THREE

Touching During
and After Childbirth

Marshall H. Klaus
Children's Hospital Medical Center of Northern California

TOUCH FOLLOWING CHILDBIRTH

To evaluate the effects of allowing parents of full-term and premature infants to begin caring for their infants shortly after birth, we have observed the early behaviors of parents with normal and sick infants. We have also studied the effects of continuous physical and emotional support for the mother by a trained laywoman during labor. These studies involved observing the effects of holding and touching the mother during labor as well as photographing the mother first touching her premature or full-term infant. The admission of parents to the premature nursery took place so smoothly that it is easy to forget the grave concerns of the physicians and nurses whose training and years of experience had taken place in the fortress of the parent-free premature nursery.

To evaluate this behavior, we photographed 9 mothers with their premature infants during their first three visits into the premature nursery and compared their behavior with 12 mothers of healthy full-term infants on their first contact. We photographed the first 10 minutes of maternal and infant behavior at 1 frame/second.

On their first visits to the nursery, mothers of premature infants touched very little, and most of their contact was on the extremities

19

of their infants with their fingertips. They spent most of their time poking the extremities, with very little contact time on the trunk of the baby (see Fig. 3.1; M. H. Klaus, Kennell, Plum, & Zuehlke, 1970).

The first contact for the mothers of the full-term infants was in privacy, with their nude infant placed next to them and a heat panel over both of them to keep them warm. A camera documented the first 10 minutes of contact at 1 frame/second, and we recorded what the mother said, using a tape recorder. During the first 3 minutes, the 12 mothers touched their babies' arms and legs with their fingertips; during the next 3 minutes they changed over to an equal amount of palm contact on the trunk of the infant. During the last 3 minutes, they mainly touched the trunk and head. What they said was even more interesting. Eighty-five percent of the mother's verbal content was related to the infant's eyes: "Please look at me," "Please open your eyes," or "Please look into my face, and then I'll know you'll love me." They appeared to need a response from the baby (see Figs. 3.2 and 3.3).

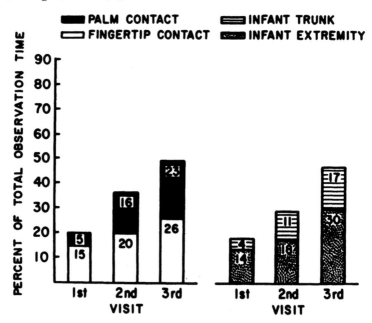

FIG. 3.1. Palm and fingertip contact on the trunk and extremities at the first three visits of 9 mothers of premature infants (from M. H. Klaus et al., 1970: *Pediatrics,* 46:187–192).

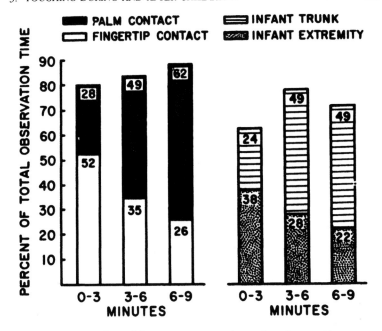

FIG. 3.2. Palm and fingertip contact on the trunk and extremities at the first postnatal contact in 12 mothers of full-term infants (from M. H. Klaus et al., 1970: *Pediatrics,* 46:187–192).

Fortunately, at this time, Prechtl and Beintema (1964) in Holland and Wolff (1959) in Boston were defining the six states of consciousness, and Emde, Swedburg, and Suzuki (1979) observed that, in the first hour of life the human infant was in the quiet–alert state for an average of 43 minutes. The infant behavior in State 4, the quiet–alert state of consciousness, is ideal for this first meeting of the mother and infant. The mother is most interested in the eyes of the infant, and in State 4 the infant is able to quietly observe her face, making possible the beginning of a reciprocal interaction.

It should be emphasized that the behavior of the mother was altered when anyone entered the room. The touching and verbal behaviors were mainly noted when the mother and infant were alone. This appears to be a private affair, although traces of these behaviors are seen in a busy delivery room. It was unclear whether these differences between the mothers of premature and full-term infants were due to what the mothers of premature infants had been told about their babies, the physical barrier presented by the incubator, or

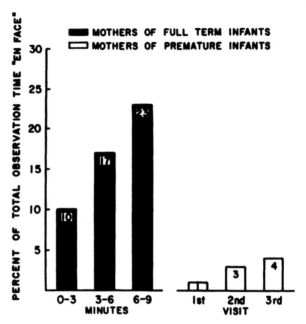

FIG. 3.3. The percentage of *en face* position recorded during the first visit of 12 mothers of full-term infants and the first three visits of 9 mothers of premature infants (from M. H. Klaus et al., 1970: *Pediatrics*, 46:187–192).

the babies' small size and appearance. To examine these questions, we next studied the behavior of mothers of small premature infants who were permitted to touch their infants in a similar fashion to the mothers of full-terms. The premature infants selected weighed about 1500 grams and had no respiratory problems. They were placed in their mothers' beds within the first day or two of life, and a neonatal nurse stayed behind the mother on a stool in case the neonate required any care. The premature infant was nude, and a heat panel above the mother's bed was servo-controlled to maintain the infant's temperature. With this arrangement there was a large increase in the time the mother was touching the infant, and even on the first visit, there was an appreciable amount of palm contact on the infant's trunk, although fingertip touching of the extremities took up a majority of the time. Bringing the premature infant to the mother significantly increased her physical contact with her infant, and touching the infant's trunk occurred more rapidly (M. H. Klaus & Kennell, 1982). When mothers visited their premature infants in the nursery (when the babies were still in incubators), the parents rarely spoke to them. However, when the premature infants were in the mothers' beds, vocalizations occurred almost 40% of the time in the first and second visits. By the second visit, 40% of the mothers were attempting to elicit a response from their infants. They also moved the infant closer for more body contact.

Rodholm and Larsson (1979) observed initial father–infant interactions of 15 fathers of full-term babies delivered by Cesarean birth. The naked infant was presented to the father 15 minutes after birth, and photographs were taken every second. An orderly progression of behavior was noted among fathers, too. The father began by touching the baby's extremities with his fingertips and then proceeded to use his palms and finally the dorsal side of his fingers. An increase in eye-to-eye contact was also observed. The percentages of various behaviors were remarkably similar to those previously described in mothers. The investigators also observed that unrelated adults (medical students) had a touching sequence similar to that of fathers. Is this sequence the process by which humans approach an infant? Is it genetically built into our biology? Or is it just how adults approach small objects?

Lang (1972) observed that in most home births, immediately after the birth of the baby, but before delivery of the placenta, the mother picked up the baby and held him in the *en face* position while speaking to him in a high-pitched voice. Are these behaviors species specific?

Emotional and Physical Support During Labor

Our work in this area began when one of our medical students failed to follow the instructions for another study. She was only supposed to obtain the approval of primiparous, healthy mothers in early labor. They were then to go through the usual hospital routine, and the study was to begin at their babies' birth. She obtained the approval for the study early in labor, but stayed with each of 10 study mothers giving emotional and physical support until they delivered (family support was not permitted in this hospital). When we first heard about this error, we were upset, because all of these mothers and babies had to be removed from the ongoing study. However, when we looked more closely at the charts of these mothers, we found that they had unusually short labors. Surprisingly, three of these mothers delivered in the bed. This was unheard of in this hospital, because the focus of the delivery unit was sterility, and the rules of the hospital were that every mother was to deliver in a "sterile" delivery room. It is this serendipitous observation of altered labor with emotional support that has been the focus of our research for the last 10 years.

In the studies I describe, continuous emotional support was provided by a caring laywoman that we have called a *childbirth doula*. We chose the Greek word *doula*, which means "a woman caregiver of another woman." Dana Raphael (1976) first used the word to describe experienced women who helped mothers with their breastfeeding. All childbirth doulas go through a 2- to 3-week training period to teach them to be able to give the laboring woman and her partner both emotional and physical support throughout labor. The doula never leaves the mother during labor. She stays with the mother, touches and holds the mother, and explains to the mother what is going on during the labor. She also praises and reassures the mother and gives strong physical and emotional support. She always moves at the mother's pace.

The doula frees the father from being the sole support of his wife, with the associated anxiety of that responsibility, and allows him to respond during the labor in a more natural fashion. It is our experience that, because of his close emotional ties, a male partner is often limited in his ability to meet both his and the mother's needs at this intense time. One father noted to us, "I didn't realize until later how frightened and angry I felt at the staff for being left alone with my wife when we were having our first baby." Dr. Martin Greenberg noted, "The mother has a biologically-based task which is driven by a time clock, while the father feels like he's floating in air without a connection, uncertain about his tasks" (M. H. Klaus, Kennell, & P. Klaus, 1993).

One sometimes gets the impression from childbirth classes that, after seeing a few exercises, the father can become the main source of support and knowledge of the entire labor when the nurse is unavailable. Although this may be true for some fathers, many lack the skill to be effective sources of support during labor and delivery. We suggest a different, but equally important, role for the father, that of emotional support at his own pace.

To date, five separate randomized trials have evaluated the effectiveness of the doula. Table 3.1 lists the details of these five studies.

TABLE 3.1

Effect of Social Support: Five Randomized Clinical Trials

Author, Year and Location	Sample Size	Selection Criteria	Findings Exp. vs. Control (significant results only)
Sosa et al. (1980) Guatemala	n = 127 Exp = 32 Control = 95	Women aged 13–34; nulliparous; single gestation term; uncomplicated pregnancy; 1–2 cm cervical dilatation at entry	Decreased perinatal problems; decreased length of labor; increased responsiveness to infant
Klaus et al. (1986) Guatemala	n = 417 Exp = 168 Control = 249	Women aged 13–34; nulliparous; single gestation term; uncomplicated pregnancy; 3–4 cm cervical dilatation at entry	Decreased Cesarean section rate; decreased length of labor; decreased oxytocin use; decreased perinatal problems
Hodnett & Osborn (1989) Canada (urban)	n = 103 Exp = 49 Control = 54	No age specified; uncomplicated pregnancy; women enrolled in childbirth classes with partner	Increased oxytocin use; decreased need for epidural
Kennell et al. (1991) USA (urban)	n = 416 Exp = 212 Control = 204	Women ages 16–36; nulliparous; single gestation term; uncomplicated pregnancy; 3–4 cm dilatation at entry	Decreased Cesarean section rate; decreased need for epidural; decreased oxytocin use; decreased use of forceps; less maternal fever; decreased length of labor
Hofmeyer et al. (1991) South Africa	n = 189 Exp = 92 Control = 97	No age specified; nulliparous; single gestation term; uncomplicated pregnancy; less than 6 cm cervical dilatation at entry	Increased coping during labor; increased breast-feeding; lower perceptions of pain; decreased state anxiety and depression after 6 weeks

In all five studies, the mothers were healthy nulliparous women at term who had had a normal pregnancy (Hodnett & Osborn, 1989; Hofmeyer, Nikodem, & Wolman, 1991; Kennell, Klaus, McGrath et al., 1991; Klaus, Kennell, Robertson, & Sosa, 1986; Sosa, Kennell, Klaus, et al., 1980). The intervention was the introduction of a trained laywoman who provided emotional support consisting of praise, reassurance, and actions to improve the comfort of the mother, as well as an explanation of what was happening during the labor. In these studies, the doula never left the mother. The control mothers received the traditional hospital care. When the results of these five studies are combined using a meta-analysis, the presence of the doula reduced the overall section rate by 50%, the length of labor by 25%, oxytocin use by 40%, the need for pain medications by 30%, the need for forceps by 40%, and the requests for epidurals by 60%. How can we explain these findings? R. P. Lederman, E. Lederman, Work, and McCann (1978) have observed that, with an increase in maternal anxiety, there are raised blood levels of epinephrine and no-repinephrine, which are known to decrease uterine contractions. It is possible that the continuous presence of the doula reduces maternal anxiety and prevents an increase in epinephrine or norepinephrine, thus allowing the labor to progress in a normal fashion and decreasing the total length of labor. With shortened labors, there is a reduced Cesarean section rate.

In regard to the effects of doula support during labor on the mother's behavior and attitude after delivery, a hint of some of the effects were first noted in our initial study of the effects of a doula (Sosa et al., 1980). Through a one-way mirror, an observer recorded the initial behaviors of mothers with their babies after leaving the delivery room during the first 25 minutes after birth. The observer was blinded to the care the mothers received during labor. The doula mothers demonstrated significantly more affectionate interaction with their infants, showing significantly more smiling, talking, and stroking than the mothers who did not have a doula.

It is especially useful to focus on the South African study (Hofmeyer et al., 1991) which was the only study to follow the mothers for 6 weeks. The results revealed favorable effects of constant support on the subsequent psychological health of the women. At 24 hours, the mothers in the doula group had significantly less anxiety compared with the no-doula group, and fewer doula-supported mothers considered the labor and delivery to have been difficult.

The doula mothers noted that it took an average of 2.9 days for them to develop a relationship with their baby compared to 9.8 days for the no-doula mothers. Mothers in the doula groups were significantly less anxious at 6 weeks; they also scored significantly lower on the depression scale than the control group and exhibited significantly higher levels of self-esteem. At 6 weeks a significantly greater proportion of women in the doula group were breast-feeding (51% vs. 29%) and demand feeding (81% vs. 47%), and there were significantly fewer feeding problems in the doula group (16% vs. 63% in the no-doula group). Mothers in the doula group said that during the first 6 weeks after delivery they spent 1.7 hours a week away from their baby, in contrast to those in the no-doula group who spent 6.6 hours away. Of special interest is the fact that more mothers who had a doula felt satisfied with their partners at 6 weeks postpartum (85% vs. 49%) and felt that their babies were better than the standard baby: more beautiful, more clever, and easier to manage than the control mothers, who perceived their babies as just slightly less attractive than the standard infant.

Lastly, I want to describe the care in the National Maternity Hospital in Ireland, one of the few units in the Western world where continuous emotional support by an experienced woman has been part of the routine care procedures for the past 20 years. The system they use in labor is called the "Active Management of Labor." This process involves understanding the progression of labor, the woman, and her family, and then organizing the mother's experiences in the hospital. When the diagnosis of labor is made, each woman is assigned her personal nurse-midwife (usually a nurse in training to become a midwife) who remains with her throughout her labor, providing one-to-one care. Because the continuous care by the midwife appears to be one of the critical elements of this method and has often been left out of the procedures when it is transferred to another unit, it is useful to quote the originators of this procedure: "Mere physical presence is not enough. The nurse-midwife must appreciate that her primary duty to the mother is to provide the emotional support so badly needed at this critical time and not simply to record vital signs in a detached manner. A guarantee is given to every expectant woman who attends this hospital that she will have a personal nurse throughout the labor from the time of her admission to her birth without regard to the hour of the day or the night the baby is born" (O'Driscoll, Meagher, & Boylan,

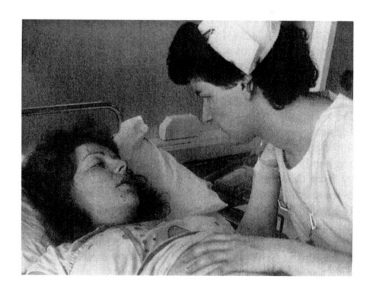

FIG. 3.4. The midwife aligns her face with the mother's (*en face*) and holds her for full support (from M. H. Klaus et al., 1993).

1993, p. 79). The nurse-midwife is trained to touch the mother, to have eye-to-eye contact and hand contact, and to use the *en face* position. In this hospital, the mean length of labor for primiparous mothers is 5.9 hours. Because of the remarkable shortening of labor, every student-midwife now delivers 225 babies per year; before this system was inaugurated, they averaged 95 babies per year. Figure 3.5 shows the close contact between the nurse and the mother near the end of labor. Interestingly, the Cesarean section rate from 1980 to 1990 remained between 5% and 6.5%, with an appropriately low neonatal mortality and morbidity. Another aspect of the acute management of labor includes rupturing the membranes when the head is engaged if the cervical dilation is slower than 1 cm/hour. If dilation of the cervix is still not at this rate, oxytocin is given. At present, only 30% of women require augmentation with oxytocin. Because rupturing the membranes appears to shorten labor by only 20 to 30 minutes, and only about 30% of mothers received oxytocin, it is fair to conclude that the one-to-one care by the nurse-midwife accounts for a major part of their good results.

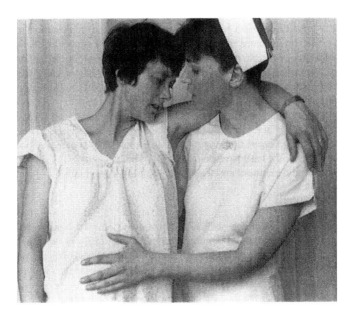

FIG. 3.5. A mother late in labor at the National Maternity Hospital in Ireland (from M. H. Klaus et al., 1993).

In trying to understand what is going on for the mother, the work of Winnicott (1987) has been helpful. He discusses the holding environment the mother makes for the baby and how important this is for the physical and emotional growth of the baby. "The baby's development cannot take place except in relation to the human reliability of the holding and handling" (pp. 96–97). I suggest that the doula produces this holding environment for the mother. She holds the mother through a physiological process during a period in which she cannot control herself. Holding the mother is a strong metaphor for what the mother does for the baby. What is important about this role is that the mother is being mothered, the mother is being held, and there is a possibility in our society, in a sense, to re-mother the mother. Is it possible that we may have the ability to internally change a woman who has had poor mothering? Is this a way to renew women who have had a difficult life history?

In *Mothering the Mother: How a Doula Can Help You Have a Shorter, Easier, Healthier Birth* (M. H. Klaus, Kennell, & P. Klaus, 1993), my wife, Phyllis Klaus, helps us to understand the process:

A doula often instinctively feels the need to mother the mother at this vulnerable time when a woman is unusually dependent and open as she prepares to move through a major maturational change in labor, delivery and becoming a parent. However, while dependent, a mother still needs the freedom to turn into herself—to take charge at an instinctual level in response to what her body wants to do. It is a paradox, really. A woman in labor needs total support—in order to let go completely, to allow her own system to adapt and respond to the power of the birthing process. This mixed need can be confusing to the mother herself and may be difficult for others to appreciate. Often caregivers find it hard to understand this complex balance: the mother's need to be dependent and independent at the same time.

She also noted:

Feeling completely safe with another human being creates a certain freedom where one can begin to test the limits of one's own capacities, begin to experience capacities probably not recognized or perhaps recognized but not risked. This freedom to be one's true self creates a feeling of creativity.

A woman, after having a doula in one of our studies, noted, "Your staying with me all this time and your total support at the same time, trusting me completely, gave me a sense of knowing that I was strong enough to handle anything in my life."

Women-helping-women in labor is an ancient and widespread practice. We reviewed anthropologic data for 128 non-industrialized hunting and gathering and agricultural societies, and all but one offered mothers continuous support during labor and delivery. When, in this country, birth shifted its location from home to hospital 70 years ago, many childbirth practices that evolved over centuries were lost or altered, including birth position and companionship during labor. In the past, it was common for a woman in labor to always be supported by other women. When American obstetrics moved birth from the home into the hospital and left out the continuous emotional support by another woman, this was a major error. We must bring back the laywoman doula in our society. I hope that, by the year 2000, continuous social support during labor and a holding environment is given to every mother in our country.

Unfortunately, we have only one study that followed mothers after discharge from the hospital. Because the results of this well-designed study were unusually intriguing, we must have further research to determine how significant labor support is in altering later maternal behavior. Is it possible that, in the future, we will have to record in all parenting studies how the mothers were cared for during labor? Only further research will determine how significant a metaphor labor support is in determining parental behavior.

Marshall Klaus—Question and Answer Session

QUESTION: A point I think you are making, to make it a little clearer, is that it is not a holding environment per se, but a contingent holding environment. What the doula is doing is responding contingently, and I think that that is a point that needs to be carefully spoken about, because I would be willing to bet that the reason why the moms are better with their infants after birth is because they get this beautiful model of when to respond and when not to respond, not only when to hold and to touch, but when to look and when to verbalize, and because they have that model from the moment the baby is born they can say, "Ok what you have been doing for me is contingently responding to me and I am now going to respond contingently to my newborn." So if we focus on the contingency, Jeff Pickens has been talking about it being a mobile biofeedback unit with the doula or the mother to the child, giving this immediate biofeedback to the mother or the baby, and that contingency is the crux of the support system.

ANSWER: I agree there is no formula; it's to meet the mother's needs. I would like to say that we have made another error when we ask the father to be the sole support of his wife. We have made a fundamental error with the father when we give him all this weighty responsibility. He should be there and he is helped greatly by the presence of the doula. For example, when the father sees more bleeding from the mother, and the mother asks if there is something wrong and should she go for the nurse, the father may say, "Oh, this is of concern." However, the doula can say, "Things are going well. The cervix is dilating. You're moving nicely. You're just bleeding a little." So, two people can have quite different responses.

QUESTION: It strikes me that contingency can be important, but there is something about touch, I would guess, which is, in itself, important. So, to focus on contingencies with all the cognitive aspects that go with it, is not at all what it is about and I am wondering why you responded this way.

ANSWER: I was delighted when he talked about meeting the mother's needs, I was thinking about it in regard to figuring out what was pleasing to the mother. There are certain mothers who, when the doula is touching them, feel no pain. They could completely tell the difference between a partner's touch and the doula's touch—they were quite different. So, touch for some mothers was terribly important.

REFERENCES

Emde, R. N., Swedburg, J., & Suzuki, R. (1979). Human wakefulness and ecologic rhythms after birth. *Archives of General Psychology, 32*, 780–783.

Hodnett, E. D., & Osborn, R. (1989). Effect of continuous intrapartum professional support on childbirth outcomes. *Research in Nursing and Health, 12*, 289–297.

Hofmeyer, G. J., Nikodem, V. C., & Wolman, W. L. (1991). Companionship to modify the clinical birth environment: Effects on progress and perceptions of labor and breastfeeding. *British Journal of Obstetrics and Gynaecology, 98*, 756–764.

Kennell, J. H., Klaus, M. H., McGrath, S., Robertson, S. S., & Hinkley, C. W. (1991). Continuous emotional support during labor in a U.S. hospital. *Journal of the American Medical Association, 265*, 2197–2201.

Klaus, M. H., & Kennell, J. H. (1982). *Parent–infant bonding*. St. Louis: Mosby.

Klaus, M. H., Kennell, J. H., & Klaus, P. (1993). *Mothering the mother: How a doula can help you have a shorter, easier and healthier birth*. Reading, MA: Addison-Wesley.

Klaus, M. H., Kennell, J. H., Plum, N., & Zuehlke, S. (1970). Human maternal behavior at first contact with her young. *Pediatrics, 46*, 187–192.

Klaus, M. H., Kennell, J. H., Robertson, S., & Sosa, R. (1989). Effects of social support during parturition on maternal and infant morbidity. *British Medical Journal, 293*, 585–587.

Lang, R. (1972). *Birth book*. Ben Lomond, CA: Genesis Press.

Lederman, R. P., Lederman, E., Work, B. A., & McCann, D. S. (1978). The relationship of maternal anxiety, plasma catecholamines, and plasma cortisol to progress in labor. *American Journal of Obstetrics and Gynecology, 132*, 495–500.

O'Driscoll, K., Meagher, D., & Boylan, P. (Eds.). (1993). *Active management of labor*. St. Louis, MO: Mosby.

Prechtl, H. F. R., & Beintema, D. (1964). Neurological examination of the full-term and newborn infant. *Clinical Developments in Medicine* (London), *12*.

Raphael, D. (1976). *The tender gift: Breastfeeding*. Englewood Cliffs, NJ: Prentice-Hall.

Rodholm, H., & Larsson, K. (1979). Father–infant interaction at the first contact after delivery. *Early Human Development, 3*, 21–27.

Sosa, R., Kennell, J. H., Klaus, M. H., Robertson, S., et al. (1980). The effect of a supportive companion on perinatal problems, length of labor and mother–infant interaction. *New England Journal of Medicine, 303,* 597–600.

Winnicott, D. W. (1987). *Babies and their mothers.* Reading, MA: Addison-Wesley.

Wolff, P. H. (1959). Observations of newborn infants. *Psychosomatic Medicine, 21,* 110–118.

CHAPTER FOUR

Touch and the Kangaroo Care Method

Gene Cranston Anderson
Case Western Reserve University

Kangaroo care is not touch alone. It involves the familiar maternal milieu, which is the ideal ecological niche for the newborn infant (Anderson, 1977), and it is energy-conserving (Ludington, 1990). But without touch there could be no kangaroo care.

Most people have at least heard about skin-to-skin contact for preterm infants, otherwise known as *kangaroo care*. With this method, which originated in Bogotá, Colombia, the mother holds the diaper-clad infant beneath her clothing skin-to-skin and upright between her breasts or on one breast. This kind of care has been affectionately named *kangaroo care*, because it resembles the way that marsupials care for their young. Some people do not like this name, but the reality is that it is used around the world, by those who study it, those who implement it, and those who promote it at the policy level (e.g., UNICEF and WHO).

In complete kangaroo care, the mother allows self-regulatory access to breastfeeding. Fathers hold their infants skin-to-skin, also. Kangaroo care can be practiced in varying degrees. The variations occur along several continua: how soon it begins, how often it is given, how long it is given, and how completely it is given (i.e., if breastfeeding is done at all and how much). The decision to begin kangaroo care also varies according to gestational age, birth weight, postnatal age, and severity of illness. To facilitate description, I have developed five categories, based primarily on how soon kangaroo care begins.

CATEGORIES OF KANGAROO CARE

Late Kangaroo Care

The most common category in the United States is called *late kangaroo care*, which begins when the infant is relatively stable, usually breathing room air, and almost ready to go home. Late kangaroo care also includes the infant who has been very ill. The first infant to receive kangaroo care at the University of Florida was a 23-week-gestation infant who had developed bronchopulmonary dysplasia. When kangaroo care began at 35 weeks postconceptional age (12 weeks postbirth), she was still receiving oxygen, but was almost ready to go home, oxygen and all (see Fig. 4.1).

Intermediate Kangaroo Care

With *intermediate kangaroo care*, the infant has completed the early intensive care phase, but usually still needs oxygen and probably has some apnea and bradycardia. Intermediate care also includes infants

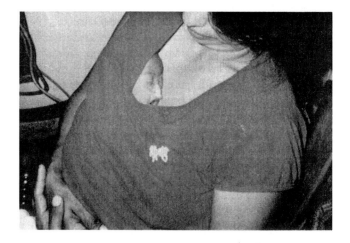

FIG. 4.1. This infant was born after 23 weeks gestation. She was about 38 weeks postconceptional age in this picture and was discharged home soon after this picture was taken.

who are stabilized with the aid of a ventilator (Gale, Franck, & Lund, 1993; Gloppestad, 1987). Another way to give intermediate kangaroo care is to place a weak preterm infant at the breast during gavage feedings. This is an excellent way to stimulate milk production, and gives the infants beginning experiences, when they are still too weak to breast-feed very much. (Lennart Nilsson, the famous Swedish photographer, has included a beautiful picture of this method in the latest edition of his impressive book on fetal development and the early time after birth; 1990.)

Early Kangaroo Care

The next category is *early kangaroo care*, for infants who are easily stabilized; this can begin the first day, or even during the first few hours after birth. In Fig. 4.2a a Colombian infant is breast-feeding 8 hours after birth. This infant was born after 32 weeks gestation, weighing 1850 grams, and had an Apgar of 6 at 1 minute. He was ready for discharge 36 hours after birth. I saw this infant in Bogotá, and he was my first experience with kangaroo care. When I saw him 2 years later (Fig. 4.2b), he was obviously healthy.

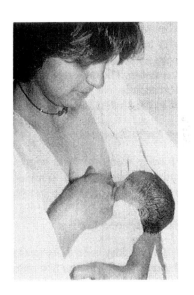

FIG. 4.2a. This Colombian infant, born after 32 weeks gestation, weighing 1850 grams, is breast-feeding during kangaroo care 8 hours postbirth. (Photograph by Libby Marks.)

FIG. 4.2b. The infant in Fig. 4.2a is seen here 2 years later at home with his older brother and younger sister. (Photograph by Libby Marks.)

In Bogotá, stabilization for preterm infants who have an Apgar of 7–10 at birth is accomplished by laying the infant prone in a warm incubator and allowing it to rest. If the Apgar is 4–6, the infant is placed prone in a warm incubator and given some oxygen; it may also be given intravenous fluids. Infants who are reasonably healthy at birth can be stabilized relatively easily using this minimal technology. This kind of infant, however, cannot sustain stability very well when alone. The secret is to return the infant to the mother, skin-to-skin, as soon as it is stable. The mother can help the infant to maintain this stability. Unfortunately, we usually miss this brief window of opportunity, at least in the United States.

Very Early Kangaroo Care

Very early kangaroo care begins in the delivery or recovery room, usually between 30 and 40 minutes postbirth (Fig. 4.3). In this category, the mother helps to stabilize her infant.

Birth Kangaroo Care

The last category is *birth kangaroo care*, where the infant is returned to the mother during the first minute after birth. I consider this ideal. If the mother is lying down, the infant is simply placed prone near her breasts. If the mother has given birth in a semi-squatting position,

FIG. 4.3. This mother is giving kangaroo care at the University of Florida to her 34-gestational-week infant, about 45 minutes after his birth.

she sits down cross-legged and picks her infant up and holds it. This latter method is recommended by Michel Odent, the obstetrician from Pithiviers, France, who is one of the forerunners of kangaroo care (Odent, 1984). He told me that the sitting-down cross-legged position is a very healthy one for the mother immediately after birth, especially if she is holding her infant (M. Odent, personal communication, June 12, 1988).

The last 100 consecutive infants who were born in Dr. Odent's program at Pithiviers in the 1970s and 1980s and weighed less than 2500 grams at birth averaged 2300 grams, ranging from 1600 to 2490 grams. With Dr. Odent's method of care, first the mother held her infant skin-to-skin while she was sitting on the floor. After the placenta was delivered, she went to her room, her infant accompanying her in an incubator placed next to her bed. Here, she could breastfeed her infant in a self-regulatory way. Dr. Odent had an extraordinary record with these babies, in terms of outcome. All were discharged between 2 and 16 days after birth (an average of 8 days). Only one death occurred, and that was a 2300-gram infant. (The cause remained unknown, because the parents did not want their infant to have an autopsy.) Dr. Odent was able to follow the first 48 infants before he moved to London. He found healthy development in all of them, with none having to be rehospitalized (M. Odent, personal communication, July 27, 1988).

RESEARCH ON KANGAROO CARE

Scientific research on kangaroo care began in Bogotá. Because some methodological inadequacies had occurred, however (Whitelaw & Sleath, 1985), these reports were questioned. Since then, three randomized clinical trials have been completed in Europe and one has been conducted in the United States. Only one of these has been published to date (Whitelaw, Heisterkamp, Sleath, Acolet, & Richards, 1988), but I have summarized the results of all four trials and research with other designs in Anderson (1991). This research has provided broad support for the safety and effectiveness of kangaroo care. The infants are warm enough; they have regular heart rate and respiration; and they have adequate oxygenation, more deep sleep, more alert inactivity, less crying, no increase in infection, fewer days in incubators, greater weight gain, and earlier discharge. Lactation also increases. For example, if the mother is producing 1 cup of milk, the amount will increase to 1½ cups a day after kangaroo care begins, and this is quite a difference for the preterm infant. With kangaroo care, more mothers breast-feed, and the mothers feel more fulfilled about their pregnancy. The parents become deeply attached to their infants, and they feel confident about caring for them, even at home. Kangaroo care also promotes the normal rounded growth of the head because the infant is in an upright position, so that the head cannot be pushed into the mattress by gravity.

My colleague, Dr. Susan Ludington, made one of the most amazing findings related to kangaroo care. The infant's temperature is frequently measured with a skin probe in kangaroo care research, but Dr. Ludington suggested we measure the mother's temperature with a skin probe, as well. By doing so, we discovered a phenomenon we termed *thermal synchrony*. The first infants studied were bassinette infants who were all bottlefed. After the infants had a bottle, which was at room temperature, they started kangaroo care. What we found was a correlation for the first 10 minutes between the infant's temperature and the mother's temperature, with both temperatures increasing, first the mother's and then the infant's. What was most extraordinary was that when the infant's temperature reached the thermoneutral range, the mother's temperature would drop back toward her baseline temperature. If the infant's temperature stayed up, the mother's temperature would go all the way down to her baseline, but if the infant's temperature began to drop, the mother would warm up again, almost like a thermostat (Ludington-Hoe, Hadeed, & Anderson, 1989).

In our first kangaroo care research, we studied infants who were in bassinettes and were almost ready to go home. We used a pretest–posttest design across three inter-feeding intervals (Ludington, 1990; Ludington-Hoe, Hadeed, & Anderson, 1991). Between Feedings 1 and 2, the infants were in the bassinettes; between Feedings 2 and 3, they had kangaroo care; and between Feedings 3 and 4, they were in their bassinettes again. We continuously monitored respiration and heart rate with a pneumocardiograph. Figure 4.4a shows typical heart rate (upper tracing) and respirations (lower tracing) of an infant lying in a bassinette between feedings. Each of these samples was taken 1 hour after the end of the previous feeding. You can see that the infant is unstable. The lower tracing shows modified Valsalva maneuvers (prolonged exhalations against a partially closed glottis, which cause the face to redden and obstruct venous return) and the periodic breathing that follows. Also note the irregularity of the heartbeat and how often it approaches 100. That almost reaches the range of bradycardia, a heartbeat that is too slow. In Fig. 4.4b, you can see a dramatic difference during kangaroo care. The stability in both heart rate and respiration is extraordinary, and the heart rate is always close to what is optimal for a preterm infant. The posttest period is seen in Fig. 4.4c. The tracings are a little more stable, perhaps, and the heart rate does not go down near 100 quite so often, but the infant is essentially unstable again.

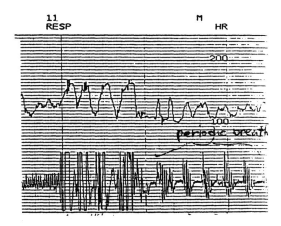

FIG. 4.4a. Pneumogram of an infant in the bassinet during pre-kangaroo care. Frequent episodes of low heart rate can be seen, as well as some crying followed by periodic breathing.

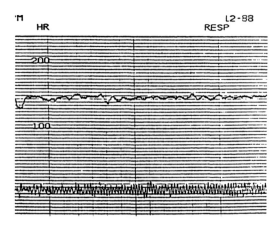

FIG. 4.4b. Pneumogram of same infant as in Fig. 4.4a being "kangarooed." Note how regular the heart rate and respirations are and that the heart rate consistently remains well above 100.

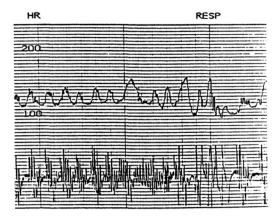

FIG. 4.4c. Pneumogram of the same infant in the bassinet again during post-kangaroo care. Heart rate and respiratory patterns are similar to those in Fig. 4.4a.

UNIVERSAL BENEFITS OF KANGAROO CARE

I predict that the benefits of kangaroo care will become recognized as universals before long. These infants quickly adopt a characteristic stress-free expression on their faces. This expression is beautiful to see, and the parents are always aware of it and are thrilled by it. I have seen this expression on the faces of preterm infants across western Europe (Anderson, 1989b), across the United States, and in Colombia; on the faces of Black infants and White infants; and on the faces of triplets, twins, and singletons (see Fig. 4.5). Perhaps this peaceful expression is, in part, a reflection of the stable physiology presented in Fig. 4.4b. This is an example of a universal.

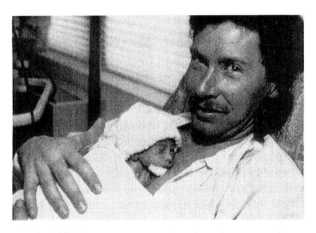

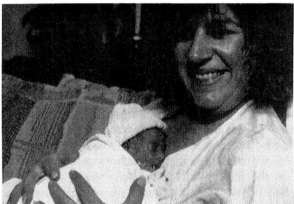

FIG. 4.5. These 11-day-old twin girls are having their first kangaroo-care experience. They were born after 31 weeks gestation, weighing 1297 and 1346 grams (appropriate in weight for their gestational age). In these pictures, they weighed 1110 and 1200 grams. The twins' parents and the nurses were amazed to see how quiet they became during kangaroo care, because they were usually very restless. (Photographs by Spencer Freeman, Florida Hospital, Orlando, FL.)

Figure 4.6 shows the weight gain of the twins in Fig. 4.5. The arrows show when kangaroo care started, and the steady weight gain thereafter is clear. I think this kind of weight gain will occur in virtually all preterm infants who are not critically ill and who have kangaroo care almost every day. This may be another universal.

KANGAROO CARE IN THE UNITED STATES

I have long had an interest in the intrauterine–extrauterine adaptation and very early kangaroo care. (In fact, my dissertation in 1973 was on just delivered newborn lambs.) Partly because of the results of that work and serendipitous findings (Anderson, 1975); partly because of the theoretical framework I developed, which involves the vagal or parasympathetic effects of touch; and partly because of the prevention possibilities, I think mother–infant separation after birth is unhealthy and unsafe (Anderson, 1989a). Therefore, I believe that the ideal time to begin kangaroo care, at least for most infants, is right after birth.

So far, my colleagues and I have studied kangaroo care beginning 30 to 40 minutes after birth, rather than at birth. We did this first in Cali, Colombia. Dr. Ludington was the person who arranged this trip, and the resulting experience was very fulfilling for me. When one of these infants began grunting in the delivery room, I knew he would ordinarily have gone right to the neonatal intensive care unit (NICU), but, because of my theoretical framework and past experience, I encouraged my colleagues to hold off and let the infant stay with his mother. So, we watched the monitors and the infant closely, and waited to see what would happen. Within 2 or 3 minutes, we could see that the infant's temperature was rising rapidly on the thermistor. His oxygen saturation was also rising rapidly. Because he was still grunting, we added oxygen. The grunting continued, nevertheless. Then we warmed and humidified the oxygen, and in 3 minutes the grunting stopped. From then on, he was essentially all right.

We had a second infant who was grunting, also, and we treated her the same way. This time, we were taking pictures. In Fig. 4.7a, this infant had just begun to feel the touch of the warmed humidified oxygen, and she is opening her eyes for the very first time. From then on, she was essentially all right (Fig. 4.7b), just like the first

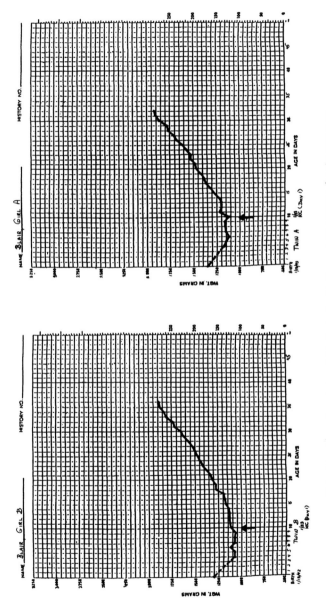

FIG. 4.6. These hospital weight charts depict the weight patterns for the twins in Fig. 4.5. Following initial weight losses, each had remained at about the same weight for the 5 days preceding kangaroo care. Both began gaining weight the day after kangaroo care began (see arrows). For the next 16 days, their average weight gain was 24.4 and 29.4 gram/day, respectively. Neonatologists consider a weight gain of 20 gram/day satisfactory; 30 gram/day is optimal. (Courtesy of Florida Hospital, Orlando, FL.)

45

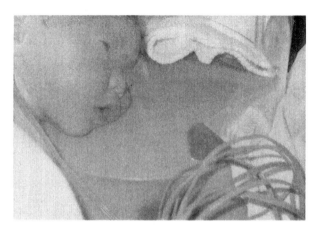

FIG. 4.7a. This Colombian mother is giving kangaroo care to her newborn infant, who has developed grunting respirations in the delivery room. Here you see the infant opening her eyes for the first time, just as the warmed and humidified oxygen began to touch her face. Audible grunting disappeared 3 minutes later. This infant was born after 34 weeks gestation and weighed 2160 grams (4⅓ lbs).

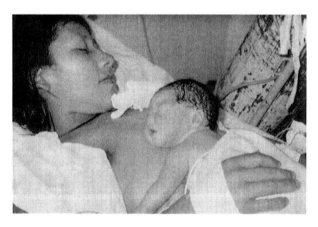

FIG. 4.7b. The infant in Figure 4.7a is now about 3 hours old. She and her mother are both sleeping. Note the stress-free expressions on their faces and their complete relaxation. Note also the full palmar touch, which is probably another universal (see also Figs. 4.1, 4.2a, and 4.5).

46

infant. These two infants went with their mothers to the postpartum ward at 6 and 8 hours after birth, respectively, and stayed there. They were fully breast-fed by the next day and were discharged 24 to 48 hours after birth. These infants were born at 34 and 36 weeks gestation, respectively. We studied four other infants who were similar, but were not grunting, and they did just as well (Ludington-Hoe et al., 1993).

The most exciting thing now is what is in progress at the University of Florida with my colleague, Brigitte Syfrett, who is a certified nurse-midwife and a graduate student. For her thesis, we are doing a small randomized clinical trial with infants born at 34 to 36 weeks gestation who are healthy at birth and whose mothers choose to breast-feed (Syfrett, Anderson, Behnke, Neu, & Hilliard, 1993a, 1993b). The intervention begins between 27 and 45 minutes after birth. We have done six infants to date, three in each group; the groups are quite comparable because of the computerized randomization technique that we are using (Conlon & Anderson, 1990).

The control infants are cared for according to hospital routine. We have stayed with the three treatment infants and their mothers continuously during the first 6 hours, and then almost continuously for another 6 hours. From then on, we check them every 15 minutes and are in the room with them much of the time. The mothers need to keep in very close skin-to-skin touch with their infants. If they do, they can help to stabilize them. The chest-to-chest position is especially effective. Their infants must stay right next to them almost all the time and the mothers need to have, and, in fact, deserve to have, excellent nursing support. The infants must be fed on cue, and some of the cues are very subtle; therefore, the mothers get help in learning to recognize and value these cues, so that the infants get fed frequently and are kept in touch with their mothers. Two of our treatment mothers have been 16 years old, one married and one not, and one was induced for severe preeclampsia, so these have not been simple cases. All three of the treatment mothers became very attentive and seemed very attached to their infants.

The three treatment infants were able to stay with their mothers (see Fig. 4.3), were thermoregulated by 18 hours, needed no supplementation, and were competent breast-feeders by 24 hours. The infants needed no help by then with breast-feeding, and the mothers had soft breasts, a full milk supply, and no nipple pain or engorgement pain. The mothers were all on Medicaid, so they were discharged by about 36 hours. Because the infants were somewhat early and small, because they were still losing weight at this point (as all preterm infants do), and because there was no follow-up program for home visitation, the physicians were unwilling to let them go home with their mothers, even though they acknowledged that the infants were healthy. We will, therefore, be using our clinical research center for our next treatment infants. The mothers and babies will stay there until 72 hours after birth. I predict that the infants will begin to gain weight by then and be able to go home with their mothers at the end of the 3 days.

On average, then, the three treatment infants were discharged in 3.7 days, having spent no time in the NICU or the step-down (intermediate) nursery. In contrast, the control infants were discharged at 10.3 days, and half of those days were in the intensive care or step-down nursery. If these lower risk preterm infants are given continuous kangaroo care beginning in the delivery room, the potential for them to grow and develop normally appears to be very real and very great. Considerable cost containment, both immediate and long term, would be an additional benefit.

Let me conclude by quoting from the preface to the third edition of Dr. Ashley Montagu's book, *Touching* (1986): "Where touching begins, there love and humanity also begin—within the first minutes following birth" (p. xv).

Gene Anderson—Question and Answer Session

QUESTION: Do you notice any culture where it is particularly difficult to promote kangaroo care?

ANSWER: Yes, this one, here in the United States. If you have a breast-feeding culture it makes a big difference. The reason why the mothers in Cali, Colombia, could go to the postpartum ward at 6–8 hours like they did with no further supervision from us, was partly because of kangaroo care. But the reason it worked so well after that on the ward and in such poor home environments is because the mothers already know how to breast-feed even if they have never had a baby themselves, because Cali is a breast-feeding culture, and the women see it all around them, so that it becomes almost second nature. The nurses in the ward were also available to help with breast-feeding problems, as were the other seven mothers in the ward. Essentially, they just assumed the mothers would breast-feed, and they all knew how to help each other. That kind of attitude seems to be what is most helpful.

QUESTION: Is there a relationship between breast-feeding cultures and touching cultures?

ANSWER: I would think so.

QUESTION: What is the frequency of duration of the kangaroo care that is being given in your various studies?

ANSWER: In the pretest–posttest studies, the duration of kangaroo care during the time between two feedings ranged from 1.5 to 2.75 hours. In the Cali study, kangaroo care was given continuously from about 30 minutes after birth to 6, 7, or 8 hours after birth. In the current study, kangaroo care begins in the delivery room 30 minutes after birth, on average, and continues until the mother is discharged, about 40 hours later. But, I am glad you asked the question for another reason. Real kangaroo care is a philosophy of care, not a one-time intervention. It's just what the mothers do. In Amsterdam, I was excited because it was the first time I had ever seen so much kangaroo care being done at once. In the step-down nursery, all 10 infants had kangaroo care and at least one parent came to be with each infant at least once during the afternoon and evening that I was there. The nurse explained, "Well, this is normal here now; this is just what we do." So that is how it can become common. We have a wonderful prototype site for this, here in the United States now, at St. Paul's Children's Hospital in St. Paul, Minnesota.

QUESTION: How many times a day is kangaroo care given? Is it 2 hours or 4 hours or what?

ANSWER: Ideally, as much as possible, at least 4 to 5 hours a day, but in the experiment by Whitelaw et al. (1988), kangaroo care was given on average only 30 minutes a day. Even so, they found significant differences, short and long term. We will need to give parents a lot of social support in this country to make it possible for them to spend many hours giving kangaroo care. We need daycare or someone to stay at home with the other children, we need to provide transportation if they don't have it, we need to make the NICU environment family friendly, and we need to protect the parents' jobs for them while they are providing this care for their babies. Based on the data coming out of the kangaroo care research, this kind of expenditure should be easy to justify. I am confident we will find that kangaroo care is not only health effective, but cost effective, when cost is measured in a long-term randomized clinical trial.

ACKNOWLEDGMENTS

My research has been supported by UNICEF; WHO; the College of Nursing and the University of Florida; numerous contributors to the Fund for Natural Care Postbirth, University of Florida Foundation; and the National Institute of Nursing Research, ROI NR 02444.

This chapter is dedicated, posthumously, to Bernice Mills for her initial contribution, which permitted me to establish the Fund for Natural Care Postbirth; for her belief in me; and for her belief in the power of natural care for mothers and their newborns.

I gratefully acknowledge my numerous colleagues worldwide, particularly those in Europe, South America, and the United States, for their contributions to the information I have gathered about kangaroo care. I am grateful, also, to the parents and infants who have taught me so much about kangaroo care, and to Myrtle Holton and Dea Kodim who provided secretarial assistance.

REFERENCES

Anderson, G. C. (1975). A preliminary report: Severe respiratory distress in two newborn lambs with recovery following nonnutritive sucking. *Journal of Nurse-Midwifery, 20,* 20–28.

Anderson, G. C. (1977). The mother and her newborn: Mutual caregivers. *Journal of Obstetric, Gynecologic and Neonatal Nursing, 6*(5), 50–57.

Anderson, G. C. (1989a). Risk in mother–infant separation postbirth. *Image: Journal of Nursing Scholarship, 21,* 196–199.

Anderson, G. C. (1989b). Skin to skin: Kangaroo care in Western Europe. *American Journal of Nursing, 89,* 662–666.

Anderson, G. C. (1991). Current overview of skin-to-skin (kangaroo) care for preterm infants. *Journal of Perinatology, 11,* 216–226.

Conlon, M., & Anderson, G. C. (1990). Three methods of random assignment: Comparison of balance achieved on potentially confounding variables. *Nursing Research, 39,* 376–379.

Gale, G., Franck, L., & Lund, C. (1993). Skin-to-skin kangaroo holding of the intubated premature infant. *Neonatal Network, 12,* 49–57.

Gloppestad, K. (1987). *From separation to closeness: Parents' experiences with closeness.* (Twenty-five minute videotape available in English or Norwegian from Kari Gloppestad, MSN, Department of Pediatrics, National Hospital, University of Oslo, Pilestredet 32, 0027 Oslo 1 NORWAY, $140.00 U.S.).

Ludington, S. M. (1990). Energy conservation during skin-to-skin contact between premature infants and their mother. *Heart & Lung, 19,* 445–451.

Ludington-Hoe, S., Hadeed, A., & Anderson, G. C. (1989, September). Maternal-neonatal thermal synchrony during skin-to-skin contact. *Abstracts of individual papers,* p. 286, Research Conference of the Council of Nurse Researchers, Chicago, IL. (Unpublished manuscript)

Ludington-Hoe, S. M., Anderson, G. C., Simpson, S., Hollingsead, A., Rey, H., Argote, L. A., & Hosseini, B. (1993). Skin-to-skin contact beginning in the delivery room for Colombian mothers and their preterm infants. *Journal of Human Lactation, 9,* 241–242.

Ludington-Hoe, S. M., Hadeed, A. J., & Anderson, G. C. (1991). Physiologic responses to skin-to-skin contact in hospitalized premature infants. *Journal of Perinatology, 11,* 19–24.

Montagu, A. (1986). *Touching: The human significance of the skin.* New York: Harper & Row.

Nilsson, L. (1990). *A child is born: The completely new edition.* New York: Delacorte.

Odent, M. (1984). *Birth reborn.* New York: Random House.

Syfrett, E. B., Anderson, G. C., Behnke, M., Neu, J., & Hilliard, M. E. (1993a, November). Early and virtually continuous kangaroo care for lower-risk preterm infants: Effect on temperature, breastfeeding, supplementation, and weight. Proceedings of the biennial conference of the Council of Nurse Researchers, American Nurses Association, Washington, DC. (Abstract)

Syfrett, E. B., Anderson, G. C., Behnke, M., Neu, J., & Hilliard, M. E. (1993, June). Kangaroo care for 34–36 week infants beginning in the delivery room: Four infants and what we learned. Proceedings of the Eighth Annual Nursing Conference in Neonatology. Kangaroo Care: Changing Times and Emerging Trends. Brigham and Women's Hospital, Boston, MA. (Abstract)

Whitelaw, A., Heisterkamp, G., Sleath, K., Acolet, D., & Richards, M. (1988). Skin-to-skin contact for very low birth weight infants and their mothers: A randomized trial of "Kangaroo Care". *Archives of Disease in Childhood, 63,* 1377–1381.

Whitelaw, A., & Sleath, K. (1985). Myth of the marsupial mother: Home care of very low birth weight babies in Bogota, Colombia. *Lancet, 1,* 1206–1208.

CHAPTER FIVE

Touch in Mother–Infant Interaction

Edward Z. Tronick
Children's Hospital, Harvard Medical School

This chapter focuses on the role of touch in the interactions of infants and young children and their caretakers. One hypothesis examined is that touch regulates both infant state and infant stress. I also explore the intriguing idea that touch conveys specific messages. For example, certain forms of touch, such as gentle holding, might convey the message, "You are safe," whereas other forms of touch, such as poking or jabbing, may convey the message, "You are physically threatened." Answers to these questions would provide us with a much more complete description of the infant–caretaker communication system. In this chapter, I present research that addresses these issues.

TOUCH AMONG THE EFE

With my colleague, Gilda Morelli (Tronick, Morelli, & Ivey, 1992), I have been carrying out a cross-cultural study of touch in a community of foragers living in Zaire. Although many view cross-cultural studies as exotic and somewhat esoteric, I believe that comparative studies are critical to our full understanding of the role of touch.

Take, for example, the variation in the amount of bodily contact experienced by the !Kung, a hunting and gathering people living in the Kalahari Desert, and American infants. Konner (1976) showed that !Kung infants were in bodily contact with someone approximately 75% of the time during the first 3 to 6 months of life, and that this level of contact started to drop off at 9 months of age. In the U.S. sample, the rate was not much higher than 30% and quickly dropped to below 25%. Without knowledge of the !Kung's level of contact, the range of variation in the amount of touch that we are aware of would be very restricted. Indeed, our knowledge in the area of touch, and for that matter in most other areas of development, is still extremely limited because of a lack of study of other communities.

For more than 10 years, our group has attempted to add to our knowledge base by carrying out a descriptive study of the development and caretaking practices of a community of foragers, the Efe, living in the Ituri Forest of Zaire (Tronick et al., 1992; Tronick, Morelli, & Winn, 1987). Like the !Kung, the Efe are a foraging population, although they live in a forest rather than a desert. The Efe[1] are a short-statured people who acquire forest foods by gathering and by hunting with bows and (mainly) metal-tipped arrows. The majority of Efe live in transient camps established in small, forested areas cleared of vegetation. Camp membership ranges from 7 to 21 people, and is composed of one or several extended families. The Efe build leaf huts that are primarily used for sleeping, food storage, and protection from inclement weather.

Most day-to-day in-camp activities take place outside the huts within the communal space, and individuals are typically in clear view of other camp members. Because the amount of time young forager children spend in the camp is considerable, ranging from 80% to 95% of daytime hours, they grow up in a community where men, women, boys, and girls are physically and visually available to them most of the time. Young children also have the opportunity to be involved in varied ongoing camp activities and to practice a variety of skills. Thus, this is a community characterized by a very high level of social contact.

---

[1]The Efe are commonly referred to in the literature as *pygmies*. We have chosen to use this term sparingly. Although the term *pygmy* is informative to the reader, it is considered pejorative by the Efe.

We gathered data on Efe life in the field using a behavioral coding system to describe the patterns of social contact and touch in this community (Tronick et al., 1992). Figure 5.1 presents data on the proportion of time the young child (from infancy to 3 years) was in direct social contact with someone. The contact might be physical, or it could be in the form of someone talking to the infant. In only about 3% of the intervals was the young infant out of contact with someone. As far as we know, this holds for evening and nighttime caretaking as well. There was a significant decline in the amount of contact from 97% to about 30%, at age 3.

Figure 5.2 presents the proportion of intervals the infant was in social contact with different individuals, such as the mother, father, and others, over the first 3 years of life. During the first year, the child had social contact with the mother approximately 50% of the time, but this dropped radically, to less than 10% of the time by age 3. "Others," a category that includes both adults and children, made up about 50% of the infant's social contact. Fathers had relatively little social contact with their infants. However, regarding the father and other men, it should be noted that fathers were out of the camp more than the mother and others because of their work, which accounts, in part, for their low level of daytime contact. In fact, preliminary observations suggest that fathers, like mothers, may be in more contact with the infants at night, and that fathers, like mothers, sleep with their infants.

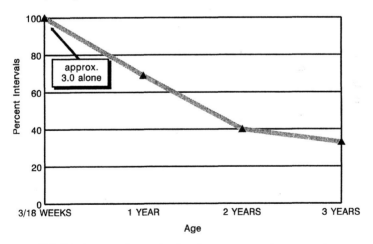

FIG. 5.1. Percent of intervals Efe infants are in social contact with any caretaker.

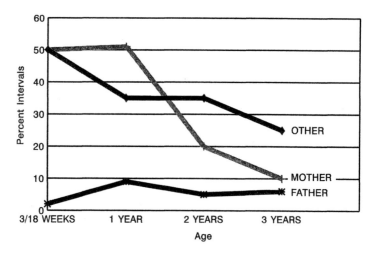

FIG. 5.2. Percent of intervals infants are in social contact with mother, father, and others.

Figure 5.3 presents data on physical contact other than holding. The data on the youngest infants provide an initial starting point for changes observed with development, although these findings may be unreliable, because discriminating physical contact that was not holding was difficult in on-going naturalistic observations. At 1 year, infants experienced physical contact during approximately 50%

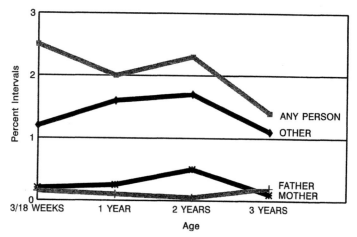

FIG. 5.3. Percent of intervals Efe infants are in incidential physical contact.

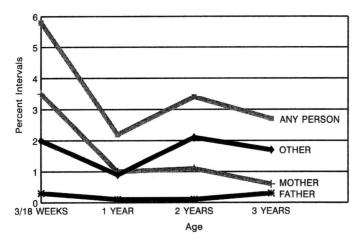

FIG. 5.4. Percent of intervals Efe infants are groomed.

of the intervals coded. The mother and others were primarily responsible for providing physical contact. Others maintained their rate of physical contact over the first, second, and third years, whereas the mother's rate decreased. Again, fathers had little physical contact with their infants relative to the mother and others.

Figures 5.4 and 5.5 present data on two specific forms of touch: grooming and affectionate touch. Grooming shows a decrease over the first year of life and then a slight increase. Others engaged in

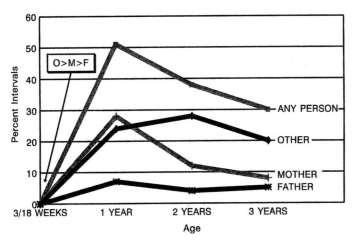

FIG. 5.5. Percent of intervals Efe infants receive affectionate touch.

a significant amount of grooming even during the newborn period, although initially the mother provided the greatest proportion of grooming. The level of grooming by others remained fairly constant over the first 3 years. Fathers did almost no grooming of their infants relative to others.

Figure 5.5 presents the data on affectionate touch. Coding of affectionate touch was based on our judgment of what "looked" affectionate and reflects our (research) community's criteria. There may have been other forms of affectionate touch that took place among the Efe that we failed to discriminate. Of course, the opposite is possible, as well. Interestingly, we found that others carried out affectionate touch with the infant at a much higher rate than the mother or the father.

In sum, among the Efe, we found not only high levels of social and physical contact, which changed with development, but also different forms of touch that were differentially distributed across different people at different developmental periods. In this society, variation in infants' experience of touch from different individuals seems to be one of the ways in which the child comes to identify different individuals. Indeed, for the Efe, and for other communities as well, to the extent that different individuals use touch in different ways than they use other modalities of communication when interacting with the infant, then to that extent may touch play a specific role in the formation and quality of the child's relationships. For example, one might imagine the Efe infant as experiencing the mother as "someone who touches me," whereas this is not the child's experience of the father. In other communities, infants would have quite different touch-defined experiences with different individuals.

There is a caveat to interpretations of data such as these. One popular hypothesis contends that foraging peoples living in tech-nologically simple societies represent the human evolutionary past in the environment of "human adaptedness." Thus, it has been ar-gued that the traditional way of doing things is more reflective of human evolutionary history—especially the forces of natural selec-tion—than are the patterns of contact and touching engaged in by more technologically advanced peoples. This suggests that the Efe way of doing things is more "natural." This line of argument is very problematic. The Efe, as individuals and as a community, have adapted to a specific social and physical ecology. These adaptations are neither more nor less biologically based than those of other cultures. That is, the Efe lifestyle is no more or less genetically based than the lifestyles of other peoples. As with other communities, Efe behaviors are environmentally contingent and influenced to the same degree by human evolutionary history.

With this argument in mind, we have suggested that the amount of touching that takes place between Efe adults and their young infants and children is fitted to a particular set of physical and social opportunities (e.g., access to other caregivers) and constraints. We have argued from the perspective of physiological ecology that Efe holding patterns facilitate the infant's achievement of thermal regulation and promote growth (Tronick et al., 1987). On the sociocultural side, we have argued that these infants are engaged in a system in which adults and other children consistently facilitate the regulation of infant behavioral organization. The extent of regulation makes the Efe infant relatively dependent on social and physical input from others in order to function normally. And to function normally as an Efe requires functioning not independently, but always in a group context, in an environment rich in physical and social interaction. Thus, the Efe pattern of touch serves as a contrast to other cultural patterns of touch, but not as a model for other societies, which face different social and physical ecological demands.

TOUCH DURING FACE-TO-FACE INTERACTIONS

In contrast to our naturalistic studies of the Efe, we have been doing laboratory studies of face-to-face interactions between mothers and infants in Boston (Tronick, 1989). In the context of these playful but structured interactions, we have been examining how much and what kind of touching takes place. Field (1984) and Kaye and Fogel (1989) have looked at similar interactions, and found that mothers touch their infants during brief social interchanges about 61% of the time. Similarly, Stack and Muir (1992) found that touch occurs about 68% of the time at 3, 6, and 9 months of age.

Figure 5.6 presents data generated in collaboration with my colleague, M. Katherine Weinberg (Weinberg, 1994). The figure shows the total amount of touch and the proportion of several types of touch—stroking, rhythmic touching, holding, tickling, kissing, poking/pinching—during face-to-face interactions between mothers and their 6-month-olds. The largest proportion of time was spent

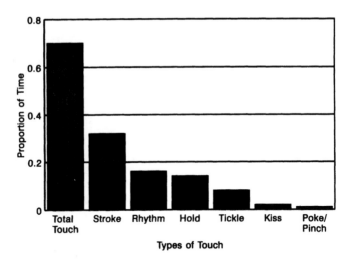

FIG. 5.6. Total amount and proportion of several types of touch.

in stroking, rhythmic touching, and holding the infant. Tickling and kissing are more discrete behaviors and took up a smaller proportion of time. All of these behaviors appear to be affectively positive. Poking and pinching are negative and occurred rarely in these interactions. Given the difference in the quality of these forms of touch, as well as their differential distribution, it may be that each of these forms of touch conveys a different message.

In research building on these data, another of my collaborators, Becky Brown, is conducting a study aimed at understanding the independent roles of touch, vision, and voice in mother–infant interaction (Brown & Tronick, in preparation). The study has five conditions: a normal play condition, in which the mother talks, touches, and vocalizes to her infant; three experimentally manipulated conditions, in which the infant only sees the mother, only hears her, or only feels her touch; and an alone condition, in which the baby is alone.

Figures 5.7–5.10 present preliminary data on infant affective and behavioral states across these conditions. In the touch-only condition, the infant reacts in an affectively and behaviorally subdued manner. The infants exhibit the lowest level of fussing or crying; a low level of scanning, which we consider a sign of stress; a high level of attention to objects; and fewer smiles than in the normal and face-only conditions.

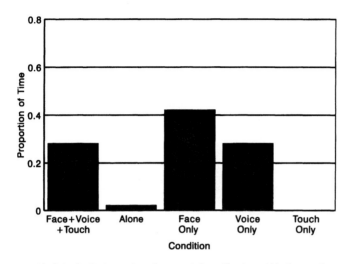

FIG. 5.7. Preliminary data showing infant affective and behavioral states.

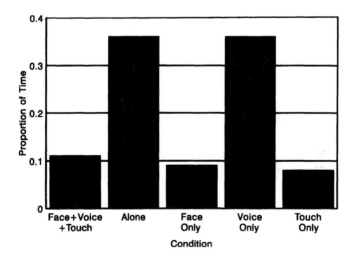

FIG. 5.8. Preliminary data showing infant affective and behavioral states.

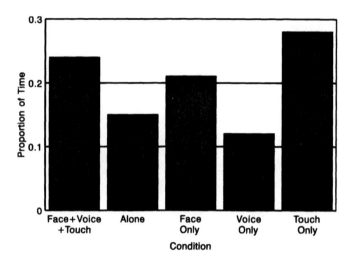

FIG. 5.9.   Preliminary data showing infant affective and behavioral states.

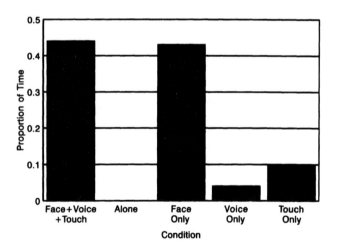

FIG. 5.10.   Preliminary data showing infant affective and behavioral states.

These findings are supported by research conducted by Stack and Muir (1992). They used Tronick's Face-to-Face Still-Face Paradigm (Tronick, Als, Adamson, Wise, & Brazelton, 1978) to evaluate the role of touch in modulating infant stress. There are three episodes in the Face-to-Face Still-Face paradigm:

1. A normal face-to-face play episode, during which the mother is instructed to play with her infant.
2. A Still-Face episode, during which the mother is instructed to hold a poker face and to be nonresponsive to the infant (i.e., not to touch, talk, or smile at the infant).
3. A reunion play episode, during which the mother is instructed to resume normal face-to-face play.

Each episode lasts 2 minutes and is separated by a 15-second interval during which the mother is instructed to turn her back to her infant.

In numerous studies, investigators have found that the Still-Face episode is stressful to the infant (e.g., Tronick et al., 1978; Stack & Muir, 1992). In a recent study, Weinberg and I found that infants express more anger and sadness during the Still-Face episode than in the first, normal play, interaction (Weinberg & Tronick, 1994). We have also found a high level of negative affect expressed during the reunion episode. Thus, to some extent the Face-to-Face Still-Face Paradigm mimics the Strange Situation, which also has a sequence of episodes of normal play, stress, and reunion. Also, as with the Strange Situation, where standard procedures are required to get comparable results, procedural variation of the Face-to-Face Still-Face Paradigm can produce perplexing results. Therefore, the standard procedure is recommended (Mayes & Carter, 1990).

Stack and Muir (1992) found that the stress of the Still-Face can be attenuated by allowing the mother to touch her infant. They found that when mothers were instructed to touch their infants during the Still-Face, infants maintained levels of smiling and attention to the environment similar to the levels seen during the normal play episode. Infants also did less fussing, crying, and grimacing during the Still-Face with touch than during the Still-Face without touch. Thus, as in Brown's (Brown & Tronick, in preparation) study, touching had the effect of calming and reducing the infant's level of stress. It appears reasonable to suggest that touch is a component of the mutual regulatory process of the caretaker–infant dyad and that it serves as an external regulator of the affective and behavioral organization of the infant (Tronick, 1989). Not every kind of touch has a facilitative regulatory effect, however.

In our studies of maternal depression, Jeff Cohn and I found that depressed mothers engage in poking and jabbing their infants (Cohn & Tronick, 1989). These behaviors are extremely rare in control mothers. Poking and jabbing were associated with infants' negative affect and gaze aversion.

In sum, we are beginning to describe different forms of touch and to examine the function of each. One hypothesis, based on the data reported here, is that several forms of touch may serve to facilitate the infant's ability to regulate his or her state. This regulatory function may be critical early in development. Later in development, touch may continue to facilitate infant in coping with stressful events and high levels of arousal. An additional hypothesis is that a particular type of touch, such as poking or stroking, can convey, in some yet to be specified manner, very specific messages to the infant and that these messages are just as specific as the messages conveyed by other forms of affective displays, such as facial expressions. Thus, touch, along with other expressive and communicative modalities, is a critical component of the mutual regulation that takes place between the caretaker and the child, and is a critical component in how the child comes to know and experience others (Tronick, 1989).

ACKNOWLEDGMENTS

Support during preparation of this chapter was provided by Grants RO3MH38300 and RO1HD22431 (PI: Edward Tronick, PhD) from the National Institute of Child Health and Development, Grants BNS-86-0913 and BNS85-06987 (PI: Edward Tronick, PhD) from the National Science Foundation, and Grants RO1MH45547 and RO1MH43398 (PI: Edward Tronick, PhD) from the National Institute of Mental Health. I gratefully acknowledge the valuable assistance of Rebecca Brown and M. Katherine Weinberg in the compilation of this manuscript.

REFERENCES

Brown, R., & Tronick, E. (in preparation). *Touch, voice, and face: Their regulatory role during mother–infant interaction.*

Cohn, J., & Tronick, E. Z. (1989). Specificity of infants' response to mothers' affective behavior. *Journal of the American Academy of Child and Adolescent Psychiatry, 28*, 242–248.

Field, T. (1984). Early interactions between infants and their postpartum depressed mothers. *Infant Behavior and Development, 7,* 517–522.

Kaye, K., & Fogel, A. (1980). The temporal structure of face-to-face communication between mothers and infants. *Developmental Psychology, 16,* 454–464.

Konner, M. J. (1976). Maternal care, infant behavior and development among the !Kung. In R. B. Lee & I. DeVore (Eds.), *Kalahari hunter-gatherers: Studies of the !Kung San and their neighbors* (pp. 218–245). Cambridge, MA: Harvard University Press.

Mayes, L. C., & Carter, A. S. (1990). Emerging social regulatory capacities as seen in the still-face situation. *Child Development, 61,* 754–763.

Stack, D., & Muir, D. (1992). Adult tactile stimulation during face-to-face interactions modulates five-month-olds' affect and attention. *Child Development, 63,* 1509–1525.

Tronick, E. Z. (1989). Emotions and emotional communication in infants. *American Psychologist, 44,* 112–119.

Tronick, E. Z., Als, H., Adamson, L., Wise, S., & Brazelton, T. B. (1978). The infant's response to entrapment between contradictory messages in face-to-face interaction. *Journal of the American Academy of Child Psychiatry, 17,* 1–13.

Tronick, E. Z., Morelli, G. A., & Ivey, P. K. (1992). The Efe forager infant and toddler's pattern of social relationships: Multiple and simultaneous. *Developmental Psychology, 28,* 568–577.

Tronick, E. Z., Morelli, G. A., & Winn, S. (1987). Multiple caretaking of Efe (Pygmy) infants. *American Anthropologist, 89,* 96–106.

Weinberg, M. K. (1994). *Different forms of touch in Tronick's Face-to-Face Still-Face Paradigm.* Manuscript in preparation.

Weinberg, M. K., & Tronick, E. Z. (1994). Affective, behavioral, and physiologic measures of the stressful nature of the reunion episode of the face-to-face still-face paradigm. *Child Development,* under review.

CHAPTER SIX

The Genetic Basis for Touch Effects

Saul Schanberg
Duke University

When my colleagues and I first published some of our work with Tiffany Field on stimulating the growth of preemies by the use of massage, I received a lot of mail from males who swore that their mothers took excellent care of them, loved them, touched them, and played with them during their development; yet they were only 5'6" tall. I tried to explain to them that we have genes which are essentially unchangeable, and that environmental inputs to the organism only regulate whether or not these genes are expressed to their fullest.

It always amazes me how long it takes scientists to recognize the obvious. Looking at the photo of Harlow's monkeys clinging together (Fig. 6.1), how can anyone doubt that a certain kind of touch enhances security and reduces anxiety? If touch is so important, one would expect that the development of these neuropsychological behaviors would be dependent on biological and molecular functions.

I would like to be able to say that, with great foresight, I designed our experiments with maternal separation (MS) in mind, but that is not the case. We were studying brain development, and were looking at certain molecular systems that are very important for maturation

FIG. 6.1. (Picture courtesy of S. J. Suomi and R. O. Dodsworth, Harlow Primate Center, University of Wisconsin)

and cell growth. What happened was that under experimental conditions in which the pups were separated from their mother, we seemed to lose our ability to measure accurately the activity of the enzyme, ornithine decarboxylase (ODC). I rechecked the assay procedure, and found it to be functioning perfectly. The search to find out what was wrong with our ODC assay led to our studies of MS.

We have learned a number of things about the biology of short-term MS using the rat as a model. Essentially, we found that if you took a rat pup away from its mother for even a short period of time, the animal would switch from one physiological state to another. We call this state the *survival mode* because the rat pup switches into a functional physiology in which energy and water is conserved and behavioral patterns are appropriate for survival in the absence of the mother.

Why conserve energy? In mammals, newborns use up most of their stored energy during delivery, so afterward they have a very low energy supply. It makes perfect sense that when the mother leaves the young (after all, she is the food storer and supplier), there would be a survival advantage for the young to go into a type of hibernation. (This should not be confused with hibernation that biologists commonly talk about, but you can think of it somewhat in that manner.)

Table 6.1 summarizes some of the physiological results of short-term MS. The variety of effects is quite interesting. The first is the marked decrease in organ tissue ODC activity. The activity of this enzyme is a well-documented index of cell differentiation and replication (Heby, 1981; Janne, Poso, & Raina, 1978; Russell, 1985). A second effect is that MS suppresses ODC gene expression normally evoked by growth hormone (GH), prolactin, or insulin. MS also induces a reduction in DNA synthesis in most organ tissues and slows insulin catabolism. Other effects of MS include increasing corticosterone secretion and decreasing GH secretion. It is important to explain why this physiological pattern would make sense under conditions of MS.

In the past, failure to thrive due to social causes was often referred to as *psychosocial dwarfism* or *non-organic failure to thrive* (Gardner, 1972). That usually meant that a failing baby would come into the hospital and be tested thoroughly. Results of these tests would be negative in terms of localizing a disease process. Under the "tender loving care" of the pediatric nurses, however, the baby would revert to normal growth patterns. When social workers sent into the home concluded that the home environment was psychosocially inadequate, the baby was given the diagnosis of non-organic failure to thrive. A team of endocrinologists at the Johns Hopkins Medical Center (Powell, Brasel, & Hansen, 1967a, 1967b; Powell, Hopwood, & Baratt, 1973), whose tests for failure-to-thrive infants included a GH release test, found that the release of GH in these children was abnormally low. After the babies were growing nor-

TABLE 6.1
Some Effects of Short-Term Maternal Deprivation

- Marked Decrease in Organ/Tissue ODC Activity and Polyamine Metabolism
- Suppression of Growth Hormone, Prolactin, and Insulin Action on ODC Expression
- Reduction in DNA Synthesis in Most Organ Tissues
- Slowing of Insulin Catabolism
- Increased Corticosterone Secretion
- Decreased Growth Hormone Secretion

mally again, a repetition of the same test revealed that the release of GH had reverted to normal. It was also occasionally noted by doctors that GH administered to failure-to-thrive babies failed to increase their growth (Rayner & Rudd, 1973).

Figure 6.2 shows the rapid time course of decreased ODC activity following separation from the mother. The action is very fast: It actually starts to decrease after only 10 to 15 minutes.

Table 6.2 illustrates that MS also leads to a severe suppression of tissue responsiveness to GH administration. Normally, GH injection leads to a fourfold increase in ODC activity. Placental lactogen, which after birth causes its induction of ODC by stimulating the GH receptor, also is without effect on ODC; however, the ODC system is very much alive, as can be seen by the action of the other drugs: It just will not react to GH receptor stimulation. This suppressive effect of MS is very specific for the growth promoting hormones: GH, prolactin, and insulin.

Another interesting effect, which is shown in Fig. 6.3, is that insulin catabolism is slowed during MS. This figure also shows something else. Rat pups have a gestation of approximately 22 days, and it is another 22 days before they are weaned. MS does not affect physiology the same way in a newborn pup and in one who is

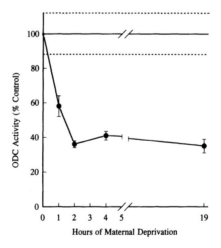

FIG. 6.2. Effect of maternal deprivation on 10-day-old rat brain ODC activity. All values expressed as mean ± S.E.M. $N = 5$ in each group. All differences significant at $p < .05$ (non-deprived value = 1.3 mμCi mg protein^{-1} 30 min^{-1}).

TABLE 6.2
Effect of Hormones on Liver ODC Activity
in Maternally Deprived Rat Pups

Drug	Dose (µg)	ODC Activity (% control)			
		Control		Deprived	
Vehicle		100 ± 22	(60)	11 ± 3	(60)†
Growth Hormone	100	437 ± 136*	(20)	11 ± 2	(20)*†
Placental Lactogen	100	315 ± 54*	(10)	10 ± 1	(10)*†
Dexamethasone	200	366 ± 62*	(10)	532 ± 51	(10)*
Dibutyryl cAMP	800	518 ± 172*	(10)	539 ± 183	(10)*
PGE-1	50	510 ± 66*	(10)	620 ± 213	(10)*

Note. 8-day-old rat pups were maternally deprived for 2 h, injected s.c. with vehicle or hormone, returned to the deprivation cages and killed 4 h later. Control pups were left with the mother and injected with vehicle or hormone at the same time. Results expressed as a percentage of control ± S.E.M. Number of animals in each group is shown in parentheses. Control ODC activity was 37 nCi 30 min^{-1} g tissue^{-1}.
*$P < 0.05$ or better relative to vehicle treated control.
†$P < 0.001$ relative to paired-control.

ready to become an adult: At 30 days of age, separation no longer affects the rat's physiology. This finding holds true for all of the effects of the MS syndrome.

Fortunately, serendipity struck again while we were studying the effects of neuropeptides endogenous to the central nervous system (CNS) on ODC activity, the polyamines, and brain development. We injected β-endorphin intracisternally (BE-IC) to observe its effects on the brain and also ran some peripheral tissue ODC assays. What we found was remarkable. Figure 6.4 shows the effects of BE-IC: ODC levels in the heart, liver, kidney, and brain were all lowered. The injection of BE-IC mimics the effects of MS, a phenomenon not duplicated by anything else we have tried. It is important to note that if the β-endorphin was injected peripherally, it had the opposite effect (it increased ODC) or no effect, indicating a CNS site of action.

We then documented that by giving a little β-endorphin centrally, we could mimic almost all of the physiological effects of MS that I have already outlined (Greer, J. V. Bartolome, & Schanberg, 1991). Because β-endorphin (an opiate receptor agonist) administered centrally induced the same physiological changes as MS, we were interested in seeing whether naloxone (an opiate receptor antagonist) could reverse some of the physiological changes induced by both

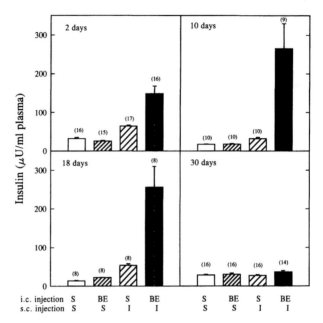

FIG. 6.3. Effect of intracisternal (i.c.) pretreatment with β-endorphin on plasma insulin concentrations in rats of different ages injected subcutaneously (s.c.) with insulin. Animals were injected i.c. with 1.5 μg β-endorphin (BE)/g brain weight (BW) 15 min before receiving 20 IU insulin (I)/kg BW, s.c., whereas control animals received matching injections of saline (S). Plasma measurements were assessed 4 hours after the second injection. Bars represent the mean ± S.E.M. of the number of determinations (given in parentheses).

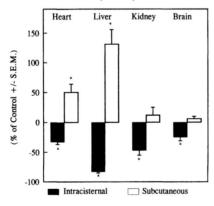

FIG. 6.4. Effects of intracisternal and subcutaneous administration of β-endorphin (1 μg) on tissue ODC activity in 6-day-old rats. Bars represent means ± S.E.M. of values from 13 to 70 animals in each group. Asterisks denote significant differences from controls ($p < .05$ or better). Control values were 1.61 ± 0.027 nmols/g/h (heart), 0.542 ± 0.053 nmols/g/h (liver), 0.325 ± 0.027 nmols/g/h (kidney), and 1.20 ± 0.07 nmols/g/h (brain).

Naloxone Reversal of MD
Effects on DNA synthesis

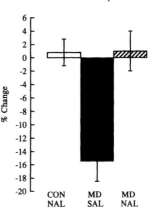

FIG. 6.5. Nine-day-old pups were injected i.c. with naloxone (NAL) or saline (SAL), and either left with their dams (control; CON) or maternally deprived (MD). Two hours later, all animals were injected s.c. with [³H] thymidine; DNA synthesis was measured 20 minutes later. Bars represent the means ± S.E.M. of values form 14–16 animals per treatment group.

MS and BE-IC. We found that it reverses similarly some of the actions of MS and BE-IC. Although DNA inhibition is reversed (Fig. 6.5), ODC suppression is not (Table 6.3). It appears that these later actions involving ODC are under the control of the *epsilon receptor*, an opiate receptor resistant to the action of naloxone (J. V. Bartolome et al., 1986; J. V. Bartolome, M. B. Bartolome, Lorber, & Schanberg, 1991).

We hypothesize, then, that β-endorphin is a central mediator of the touch deprivation syndrome. We had observed that the return of the pups to an accepting female reversed to normal all of the physiological changes induces by MS. A graduate student then solved the problem that had perplexed us for a year and a half: What sensory input signalled the presence of the mother to the pup?

TABLE 6.3
Effect of Naloxone on Liver ODC Activity in MS Pups

	ODC Activity (% control)	
	Control	Separated
Vehicle	100 ± 25	39 ± 5*
Naloxone	97 ± 20	36 ± 3*

Note. 8-day-old rat pups were injected i.c. with naloxone or vehicle and then separated or returned (control) to their dams. All pups were killed 2 h later. Results are expressed as a percentage of control ± S.E.M. Number of animals in each group 10–12.

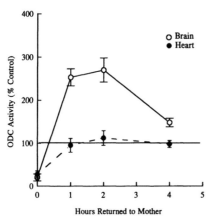

FIG. 6.6. Comparison in 10-day-old rat brain and heart of the recovery of ODC activity after a 2-hour deprivation and return to the mother. All values expressed as mean ± S.E.M. N = 5 in each group. Brain and heart values significantly below control (p < .001) after 2 hours of deprivation and no return. Brain values significantly above control and heart values (p < .05) at each point after return (non-deprived brain values = 1.3 mμ Ci^{14}CO$_2$ mg protein^{-1} 30 min^{-1}; non-deprived heart values = 5.2 m μCi^{14}CO$_2$ mg protein^{-1} 30 min^{-1}).

We knew the answer involved something the mother was doing to the pup. Dr. Gary Evoniuk studied the mother's behavior with the pups for a number of days. One day, he left the laboratory; when he came back, he had a little paint brush in his hand. He proceeded to dip the paint brush into water and "lick" the pups with a prescribed frequency and firmness of stroking. This alone will reverse the effects of MS (Evoniuk, Kuhn, & Schanberg, 1979; Pauk, Kuhn, Field, & Schanberg, 1986). Figure 6.6 shows the time course for the return of ODC levels in heart and brain following the reuniting of pup and mother. In general, tissue levels are back to normal after 2 hours.

Figure 6.7 indicates some of the kinds of touching we have tried. The only one that works is the heavy stroking pattern. The method of stroking we used could not avoid, simultaneously, partially stimulating other sensory systems that are already functioning in the pup at birth. Although hearing does not function until approximately the 9th day of age, and the eyelids do not open until the 13th or 14th day, the vestibular and kinesthetic systems, along with the tactile system, are quite functional. In Fig. 6.8, three of the effects of MS are illustrated, including the decrease in plasma GH and ODC enzyme activity levels and the increase in plasma corticosterone levels (cortisol in humans): Heavy stimulation of the vestibular or kinesthetic system did nothing to alter MS induced physiology, but the stroking pattern returned the pups' physiology to normal.

The diagram in Fig. 6.9 illustrates our working hypothesis. In this model, a decreased tactile sensory signal leads to a decrease in afferent input to the brain, which results in an increased release of

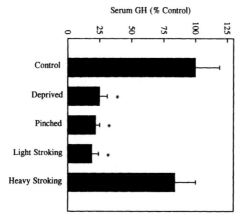

*p < .002 or better compared to controls; n > 15 except pinched and light stroking, where n > 10.

FIG. 6.7. Pups were maternally deprived and stimulated as described. Results are expressed as percent control ± S.E.M. Control serum GH = 54 ng/ml.

β-endorphin in the brain. The brain communicates to organs in the periphery in two basic ways: through nerves and through neurochemical release. It is very easy to take some organs and strip them of their nerve input or give drugs that by various mechanisms block neural transmission. In this way, we were able to show that none of the effects is neurally mediated.

Historically, scientists have been taught that almost all, if not all, neurochemicals released from the brain are routed through the pituitary gland. Perhaps this is a naive concept, because, during evolutionary development, many important neuropeptides were released by neural tissues long before there was a pituitary. It really stretches the imagination to think that everything that neural tissue was capable of releasing from its various locations must now, necessarily, be funneled through the pituitary. To establish whether the neurochemicals mediating the MS effects were released via the pituitary, we developed a surgical technique that enabled us to hypophysectomize 6-day-old rat pups in such a manner that they were not too traumatized. In order to perform our studies, we needed the pup to suckle the mother and the mother to care for the pup for at least a few days. We completed these studies. The results are shown in Fig. 6.10.

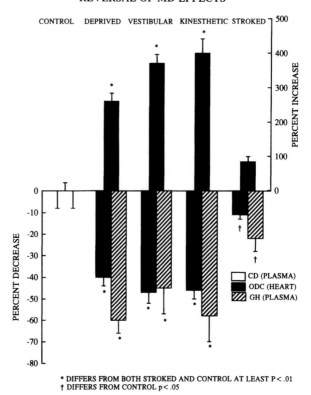

FIG. 6.8. Reversal of maternal deprivation effects. Heart ODC, serum corticosterone, and serum GH are shown as percent change from control ± S.E.M. $N = 12–15$ in each group. Control ODC activity = $1.53 ± 0.12$ nmoles/g/h. Control serum corticosterone = $3.4 ± 0.3$ ng/ml. Control serum GH = $49 ± 5$ ng/ml.

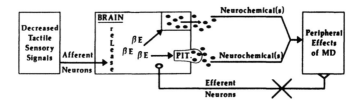

FIG. 6.9. A working model of maternal deprivation (MD). Deprivation lowers tactile sensory signals through afferent neurons, increasing the release of β-endorphins, which, in turn, trigger the release of other neurochemicals, either directly from the brain or through the pituitary, producing the peripheral effects of MD.

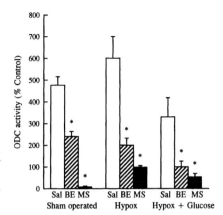

FIG. 6.10. Effects of hypophysec-
tomy (hypox) on GH induction of
lower ODC activity in 11-day-old
rats pretreated with β-endorphin or
maternal separation.

We tested the effect of MS and BE-IC on GH stimulation of ODC
in hypophysectomized (hypox) rat pups. A hypox animal has neither
GH nor a number of other hormones, so control base levels of ODC
are reduced. However, we still get stimulation with injected GH,
and it still is blocked by MS or BE-IC. Administering glucose to a
hypox pup can return much of the normal function to the system,
but the MS block of GH-induced ODC stimulation is still present.
These studies show definitively that the inhibition of GH action
caused by either MS or the central administration of BE is not mediated by neurochemical release from the pituitary.

Biologists talk a lot about gene expression, but when we observed
that tactile stimulation was facilitating growth in the preemies, we
were thinking more classically, that is, that our touching and massaging of the infant was simply changing the physiology of the neonate
so that more food would be absorbed and utilized. Recent developments in molecular biology, however, have opened new and fascinating possibilities. The brain regulates peripheral tissue functions
through neurons and neurochemicals. We know that these neurohor-
mones and neurotransmitters work on cells' surface receptors. Therefore, we can ask by what means a cell responds to the activation of a
receptor. If it wants to differentiate or replicate itself, it might
synthesize a molecule of ODC enzyme. How does it go about making
it? Well, genes can be stimulated to express RNA molecules, which
then can make specific proteins. We now know that there are different
biochemical systems capable of transducing receptor signals to genes.
There are genes that react very quickly, within 10 minutes; these are
called *immediate early genes*. These genes make certain proteins that

can influence early reacting genes, which can regulate even later reacting target genes. The signals cause a readout of the DNA of the target gene, which could be ODC, if that is what is being targeted. This is of great interest to us, because we know that the prolactin or GH molecule attaches very nicely to its receptor in the MS rat pup, and the receptor is working very well. Therefore, during MS there is something going on in the cell after the receptor is stimulated. It has been shown that certain proteins derived from immediate early genes are very involved in the regulation of ODC-gene expression. Obviously, one can hypothesize that neurochemicals released from the CNS during MS suppress the expression of the appropriate immediate early genes. If this were true, activation of the receptor by GH would not cause an induction of ODC, as it does normally. We did some preliminary experiments by preparing messenger RNA from the livers of deprived and nondeprived rat pups. Using specific probes that could identify the products of some immediate early genes, we found that MS did, indeed, significantly reduce the expression of some of these rapidly acting genes in response to prolactin administration. These experiments indicate that this type of mechanism may be involved in the brain's regulation of peripheral functions and development. I believe the brain reacting to the environment can reach its long arm right down into the middle of a cell and regulate genes that, after all, can be considered the basic units of life itself. In this regard, we must give some credit to Michelangelo, who some 450 years ago is reputed to have said, "to touch is to give life." Although I do not think he meant it in exactly the same way as I do, I think our findings are beginning to indicate that he was right.

REFERENCES

Bartolome, J. V., Bartolome, M. B., Daltner, L. A., Evans, C. J., Barchas, J. D., Kuhn, C. M., & Schanberg, S. M. (1986). Effects of β-endorphin on ornithine decarboxylase in tissues of developing rats: A potential role for this endogenous neuropeptide in the modulation of tissue growth. *Life Sciences, 38,* 2355–2362.

Bartolome, J. V., Bartolome, M. B., Lorber, B. A., & Schanberg, S. M. (1991). CNS β-endorphin regulation of insulin-induced ornithine decarboxylase expression in liver of neonatal rats. *Molecular and Cellular Neuroscience, 2,* 1–5.

Evoniuk, G., Kuhn, C., & Schanberg, S. M. (1979). The effect of tactile stimulation on serum growth hormone and tissue ornithine decarboxylase activity during maternal deprivation in rat pups. *Communications in Psychopharmacology, 3,* 363–370.

Gardner, L. I. (1972). Deprivation dwarfism. *Scientific American, 227,* 76–82.

Greer, N. L., Bartolome, J. V., & Schanberg, S. M. (1991). Further evidence for the hypothesis that beta-endorphin mediates maternal deprivation effects. *Life Sciences, 48*, 643–648.

Heby, O. (1981). Role of polyamines in the control of cell proliferation and differentiation. *Differentiation, 19*, 1–20.

Janne, J., Poso, H., & Raina, A. (1978). Polyamines in rapid growth and cancer. *Biochimica et Biophysica ACTA, 473*, 241–293.

Pauk, J., Kuhn, C. M., Field, T. M., & Schanberg, S. M. (1986). Positive effects of tactile versus kinesthetic or vestibular stimulation on neuroendocrine and ODC activity in maternally-deprived rat pups. *Life Sciences, 39*, 2081–2087.

Powell, G. F., Brasel, J. A., & Hansen, J. D. (1967a). Emotional deprivation and growth retardation simulating idiopathic hypopituitarism: I. Clinical evaluation of the syndrome. *New England Journal of Medicine, 276*, 1271–1278.

Powell, G. F., Brasel, J. A., & Hansen, J. D. (1967b). Emotional deprivation and growth retardation simulating idiopathic hypopituitarism: II. Endocrinologic evaluation of the syndrome. *New England Journal of Medicine, 276*, 1279–1283.

Powell, G. F., Hopwood, N. J., & Baratt, E. S. (1973). Growth hormone studies before and during catch-up growth in a child with emotional deprivation and short stature. *Journal of Clinical Endocrinology and Metabolism, 37*, 674–679.

Rayner, P. H., & Rudd, B. T. (1973). Emotional deprivation in three siblings associated with functional pituitary growth hormone deficiency. *Australian Paediatric Journal, 9*, 79–84.

Russell, D. H. (1985). Ornithine decarboxylase: A key regulatory enzyme in normal and neoplastic growth. *Drug Metabolism Reviews, 16*, 1–88.

CHAPTER SEVEN

Touch and Smell

Michael Leon
University of California, Irvine

A human infant comes to prefer the odor of its mother within the very first week of life (MacFarlane, 1975). My colleagues and I wondered if one is born with a preference for the odor of one's own mother's odor or whether this preference is acquired postnatally (Sullivan, Taborsky-Barbar, et al., 1991). Therefore, we presented an odor paired with tactile stimulation to infants on their first day of life, and the next day, we presented that odor off to one side. The infants' responses were videotaped, and then experimentally blind observers indicated whether the infants had turned toward the odor.

We found the following:

1. When the odor and the tactile stimulation were paired, the infant preferred the odor, as indicated by turning toward it.
2. When the tactile stimulation preceded the odor, so that the stimuli were not paired, the infants did not express a preference for the odor.
3. Odor alone or tactile stimulation alone did not increase the infants' preference for the odor.

Tactile stimulation, therefore, appears to play a critical role in the postnatal formation of an infant's preference for odors. Infants trained with one odor and tested with another had no preference for the new odor. These data indicate the specificity of the acquired preference.

To study the neurobiology of this phenomenon, we turned to another species. Rats also come to prefer the odor of their mothers (Leon, 1974), and they also come to prefer a non-maternal odor when it is paired with tactile stimulation (Coopersmith & Leon, 1984; Sullivan & Leon, 1986). Our analysis of the neural basis of this phenomenon began with a look at the first synapse at which this information was being processed in the olfactory bulb.

Olfactory receptor neurons transduce chemical information into neural information. These neurons synapse with second-order neurons in *glomeruli*, globe-like structures that surround the olfactory bulb. The glomeruli are bordered by *juxtaglomerular cells*, many of which are thought to be inhibitory interneurons. These neurons interact to modulate the *mitral cells*, which are the output neurons of the olfactory bulb. The mitral cells transmit olfactory information to the rest of the brain.

One fascinating aspect of the olfactory system is that different odors activate different regions within the glomerular layer. We can observe this differential activation by using a glucose analogue with a radioactive label on it. The more the cells work, the more glucose analogue they use. Because the analogue is not completely metabolized, it stays in the cell with its radioactive label. Therefore, the more neural activity, the more radioactivity that accumulates in glomerular-layer foci.

When a rat pup learns to prefer its mother's odor, it develops an enhanced uptake of this glucose analogue in the glomerular foci in response to its mother's odor (Sullivan et al., 1990). This indicates that we are studying the neural consequences of a natural form of learning. The pups also develop an enhanced glomerular response to nonmaternal odors that have been paired with tactile stimulation (Coopersmith & Leon, 1984; Sullivan & Leon, 1986). Tactile stimulation alone and odor experience alone are ineffective in inducing the neural or behavioral changes that the paired stimulation accomplishes.

This enhanced glomerular response is long-lived, persisting well into adulthood (Coopersmith & Leon, 1986). The response is also odor-specific: Pups trained with one odor have an enhanced response only to that odor (Coopersmith, Henderson, & Leon, 1986). In addition, there is a sensitive period for the development of the enhanced response: the first week of life (Woo & Leon, 1987).

The mechanism underlying the enhanced neural response does not involve increased respiration, and thereby, increased olfactory stimulation. Pups do not increase their respiration of this odor, and in no situation do we see a correlation between enhanced uptake of the radio-labeled glucose analogue and an increase in respiration. Because it was possible that we missed seeing a respiratory epoch that was critical for the enhanced response, we removed the ability to respire from the rats by means of tracheotomy. We then maintained a controlled airflow to their lungs and, at the same time, moved scented air rapidly through their noses to stimulate sniffs. We gave the same size and number of sniffs of the odor to the trained and control animals during the test odor exposure. Only those animals with odor preference training had the enhanced uptake of the glucose analogue in response to trained odor (Sullivan, Wilson, Kim, & Leon, 1988), indicating that differential respiration is unlikely to underlie this phenomenon.

If the enhanced glomerular response is not due to an increase in the amount of stimulation impinging on the olfactory system, maybe it is due to an intrinsic change in the neural system. We therefore looked at the olfactory bulb anatomy at this enhanced glomeruli uptake site. Trained pups have an increase of about 20% in the number of juxtaglomerular neurons in the responsive foci in the glomerular layer relative to the number present in the foci of control pups (Woo & Leon, 1991). There is no difference between trained and control pups in the number of cells present in an unactiviated region of the glomerular layer. We are studying a number of possibilities for a mechanism that could increase the number of cells in the glomerular layer.

Whatever mechanism operates here, we assume that any kind of anatomical change would involve a special response to the olfactory training on the part of the neurons. In order to monitor such a response during learning, we took advantage of the fact that juxtaglomerular neurons are dopaminergic; it is possible to monitor extracellular dopamine while these individuals are going through their training. When the pups are exposed to air, there is no change in dopamine (Coopersmith, Weihmuller, Kirstein, Marshall, & Leon,

1991). Either odor or tactile stimulation alone provokes a small rise in dopamine. There is, however, a prolonged increase of about 400% in dopamine when tactile stimulation and odor are combined. This special response evoked by the paired exposure to tactile stimulation and odor may induce the neural changes that characterize early olfactory learning.

It struck us that we might be able to see some functional changes in the way the bulb tells the rest of the brain about this learned information. Therefore, we recorded single-unit activity of the mitral cells that lie close to the responsive region of the glomerular layer (Wilson & Leon, 1988) and found that there is inhibition of the mitral cell responses to the trained odor. Mitral cells distant to the responsive region of the bulb did not have this altered response pattern to a trained odor. Early olfactory learning, therefore, changes the processing of the neural signal produced by the olfactory bulb.

Norepinephrine seems to play an important role in mediating the effects of tactile stimulation. The neonatal locus coeruleus, from which the noradrenergic neurons project massively to the bulb (McLean & Shipley, 1991), increases in activity in response to tactile stimulation (Nakamura, Kimura, & Sakaguchi, 1987). When we monitored norepinephrine levels in the bulb, we found that tactile stimulation stimulates a rise in norepinephrine (Rangel & Leon, 1994). If we block the beta-noradrenergic receptors in the pups, we block the behavioral preference, the enhanced neural response, and the suppression of the mitral cell response (Sullivan, Wilson, & Leon, 1989; Sullivan, McGaugh, & Leon, 1991). If norepinephrine mediates the activity of the tactile stimulation, we should be able to remove the tactile stimulation and, by pairing the norepinephrine with the odor, stimulate early olfactory learning. Indeed, pairing an odor with a noradrenergic agonist stimulates the behavioral preference, the enhanced neural response, and the suppression of the mitral cell response. The dose–response curve for the noradrenergic agonist describes an inverted U-shaped function: When there are very low or very high levels of norepinephrine, learning is suppressed.

There appears to be an optimal level of noradrenergic stimulation that is brought about by tactile stimulation, which provokes the development of preferences to olfactory cues early in life. A mother's touch would appear to play an important role in the development of attraction to the mother herself.

Michael Leon—Question and Answer Session

QUESTION: How may this relate to bonding? That is, putting together maternal things like odor and certain identifiers?

ANSWER: There are a number of ways that it could be involved in this. For example, in rats it turns out that they need the olfactory stimulation in which they learn about the mother's nipple in order to focus in on it and attach to it. It is quite possible that the recognition of the mother by odor plays a rather important role in bonding, and that odor may gain its importance via learning.

QUESTION: Where is this written down specifically?

ANSWER: The *Annual Review of Psychology* (1992) has a review of this work.

QUESTION: Is this true of the c-section model, or is this tied to the olfactory experience in the birth canal?

ANSWER: We think that the system that we are talking about may have important roles in late fetal life and during parturition itself because when you have compression, that is, touch of not only the fetus, but of the umbilical cord, you cut off oxygen from these individuals. When you do that, you get a massive increase of norepinephrine. Pairing odor with hypoxia actually induces a preference for the odor, perhaps due to a natural pairing of norepinephrine with odors.

QUESTION: Assume, for the moment, that the mother has given birth to the litter by c-section, and the pup is given directly to the father, so that the first series of odors are paternal odors. What effect would that have?

ANSWER: The fact that you can take an odor off the shelf and pair it with tactile stimulation and get this phenomenon suggests to me that fathers could have odors that could become attractive to the young.

ACKNOWLEDGMENT

This work was supported by the Harris Foundation and grant MH-48950.

REFERENCES

Coopersmith, R., Henderson, S. R., & Leon, M. (1986). Odor specificity of the enhanced neural response following early odor experience in rats. *Developmental Brain Research, 27,* 191–197.

Coopersmith, R., & Leon, M. (1984). Enhanced neural response following postnatal olfactory experience in Norway rats. *Science, 225,* 849–851.

Coopersmith, R., & Leon, M. (1986). Enhanced neural response by adult rats to odors experienced early in life. *Brain Research, 371,* 400–403.

Coopersmith, R., Weihmuller, F., Kirstein, C. L., Marshall, J. F., & Leon, M. (1991). Extraocular dopamine increases in the neonatal olfactory bulb during odor preference training. *Brain Research, 564,* 149–153.

Leon, M. (1974). Maternal pheromone. *Physiological Behavior, 13,* 441–453.

MacFarlane, A. J. (1975). Olfaction in the development of social preferences in the human neonate. *CIBA Foundation Symposium, 33,* 103–117.

McLean, J. H., & Shipley, M. T. (1991). Postnatal development of the noradrenergic projection from locus coeruleus to the olfactory bulb in the rat. *Journal of Comparative Neurology, 304,* 467–477.

Nakamura, S., Kimura, F., & Sakaguchi, T. (1987). Postnatal development of electrical activity in the locus coeruleus. *Journal of Neurophysiology, 58,* 510–524.

Rangel, S., Leon, J., & Leon, M. (1994). Early odor preference training increases olfactory bulb norepinephrine. *Society for Neuroscience Abstracts, 20,* 328.

Sullivan, R. M., & Leon, M. (1986). Early olfactory learning induces an enhanced olfactory bulb response in young rats. *Developmental Brain Research, 27,* 278–282.

Sullivan, R. M., McGaugh, J., & Leon, M. (1991). Norepinephrine-induced plasticity and one-trial olfactory learning in neonatal rats. *Developmental Brain Research, 60,* 219–228.

Sullivan, R. M., Taborsky-Barbar, S., Mendoza, R., Itino, A., Leon, M., Cotman, C. W., Payne, T. F., & Lott, I. (1991). Olfactory classical conditioning in neonates. *Pediatrics, 87,* 511–518.

Sullivan, R. M., Wilson, D. A., Kim, M. H., & Leon, M. (1988). Behavioral and neural correlates of postnatal olfactory conditioning: I. Effect of respiration on conditioned neural responses. *Physiology of Behavior, 44,* 85–90.

Sullivan, R. M., Wilson, D. A., & Leon, M. (1989). Norepinephrine and learning-induced plasticity in infant rat olfactory system. *Journal of Neuroscience, 9,* 3998–4006.

Sullivan, R. M., Wilson, D. A., Wong, R., Correa, A., & Leon, M. (1990). Modified behavioral and olfactory responses to maternal odors in weanling rats. *Developmental Brain Research, 53,* 243–247.

Wilson, D. A., & Leon, M. (1988). Spatial patterns of olfactory bulb single-unit responses to learned olfactory cues in young rats. *Journal of Neurophysiology, 59*, 1770–1782.

Woo, C. C., & Leon, M. (1987). Sensitive period for neural and behavioral response development to learned odors. *Developmental Brain Research, 36*, 309–313.

Woo, C. C., & Leon, M. (1991). Increase in focal population of juxtaglomerular cells in the olfactory bulb associated with early learning. *Journal of Comparative Neurology, 305*, 49–56.

CHAPTER EIGHT

Touch and the Immune System in Rhesus Monkeys

Stephen J. Suomi
National Institute of Child Health and Human Development

Rhesus monkeys, like most advanced primate species, engage in a lot of touching in their day-to-day activities. Figure 8.1 illustrates a typical family grouping of rhesus monkeys, with a mother and her newborn infant nursing and contacting the mother ventrally. A grandmother and some siblings are also involved in the scene. This is quite typical of rhesus monkey family life in both wild and captive settings. That is, these monkeys engage in a great deal of social contact in a variety of forms, and this contact has both behavioral and physiological consequences. Much of this contact is provided and initiated by the infants in their family group.

Newborn monkeys, like newborn humans, have strong grasping and clasping reflexes that can be elicited by stimulation, especially by contact with a mother's ventrum. As a result, a newborn monkey spends virtually all of its initial hours and days in ventral contact with its mother, where it not only can obtain nourishment, but also experiences what Harry Harlow many years ago termed *contact comfort* (Harlow, 1958).

Harlow showed that contact comfort was crucial for normal social emotional development (H. F. Harlow & M. K. Harlow, 1962). The contact is also highly functional for these infants from a very young

FIG. 8.1. Typical rhesus monkey multigenerational matrilineal family group.

age, because their mothers are very active in naturalistic settings; for an infant to be able to hang on while its mother is on the move is quite useful. Moreover, contact comfort does not go away entirely with age. Sometimes, older siblings get into the act as well, as illustrated in Fig. 8.2, suggesting that sibling rivalry does not have its origins in humans or, at least, is not an exclusively human characteristic.

FIG. 8.2. Older sibling clinging to mother's back while infant clings to her ventrum.

As these monkeys get older, they experience other forms of physical contact, not only from the mother but from other members of their social group. Figure 8.3 shows an older sister grooming an infant who is still receiving ventral tactile contact from its mother. In succeeding months, a rhesus monkey infant gradually breaks the bond with the mother and begins directing some of its social activities elsewhere, primarily toward peers. Nevertheless, in peer interaction, too, touch and contact are crucial, whether they occur in early forms of play or in the form of temporary care of a younger sibling.

Figure 8.4 shows a young adolescent (3-year-old) female holding her infant sibling. In about a year or so, she will be a mother herself. Perhaps she is getting some practice in this setting as well. In sum, contact is an essential part of the socialization process, and a variety of different forms of contact are important for species-normative monkey interaction from birth through the juvenile and adolescent periods of development.

When monkeys become adults, they continue to engage in tactile contact and reap a variety of social benefits. Figure 8.5 depicts a very relaxed individual. Part of his demeanor is a product of the grooming he is receiving from his partner. Of course, as can be seen in Fig. 8.6, such activities can elicit additional grooming contact, and, although this could conceivably get out of hand, in fact, such grooming "networks" are an integral feature of adult interactions.

FIG. 8.3. Grooming behavior directed toward an infant clinging to its mother.

FIG. 8.4. Ventral contact between a young adolescent female and her infant sibling.

It has now been empirically established that these types of contact are intricately connected and are passed along cross-generationally (Suomi et al., 1994).

Figure 8.7 shows a mother–daughter pair from our colony at the National Institutes of Health (NIH) animal center. About 6 months after this photo was taken, the daughter became a mother herself. We have now been able to establish, in a number of longitudinal studies looking at cross-generational phenomena, that the best predictor of the amount of time a young mother will spend with her newborn infant is the amount of time that she spent in contact with her mother when she was an infant herself. This is a finding previously reported in vervet monkeys by Fairbanks (1989), and we now have comparable data from rhesus monkeys (Suomi, Champoux, & Higley, 1994). In summary, throughout the lifespan and across generations, various kinds of contact are crucial for normal social development in rhesus monkeys.

FIG. 8.5. Adult male being groomed by consort partner.

FIG. 8.6. Rhesus monkey grooming network, reflecting social dominance hierarchy.

93

FIG. 8.7. Rhesus monkey mother–daughter pair.

The history of scientific interest in early tactile stimulation dates back to H. F. Harlow (1958), who first alerted psychology and the rest of the sciences to the importance of touch or what he called *contact comfort* in his pioneering studies with infant monkeys reared on artificial surrogates. Harlow was able to demonstrate that contact with a terrycloth-covered surrogate "mother" was more important to the infant than access to a wire "mother" that provided it with nutrition. In fact, monkey infants would solve the problem of feeding by hanging on to the cloth mother and then briefly leaning over and sipping off the wire mother, and then returning back to the cloth mother, as illustrated in Fig. 8.8.

In subsequent work, Harlow was able to show that this contact was important not only initially, but also as the infant got older, as it began to use its surrogate as a base for exploration, just like monkeys use real mothers as a base for exploration (H. F. Harlow & Zimmerman, 1959). This provided much of the basis for Bowlby's early ideas regarding attachment, especially the concept of the secure base (Bowlby, 1969). Whereas the wire surrogate had none of these characteristics or capabilities, a little bit of contact with a cloth surrogate gave the infant sufficient security for it to be able to explore toys and objects in a strange environment.

Harlow's laboratory was also the first to show the consequences of having no opportunity for touch in his studies of isolation of infants from their mother from birth onward. These infants grew up

FIG. 8.8. Infant monkey moving from cloth surrogate to obtain milk from wire surrogate.

either with or without surrogates and in the absence of social contact opportunities with other conspecifics. The consequences were devastating. Having a natural tendency to clasp onto something, and having neither surrogate nor mother to clasp onto, these monkey infants developed patterns of clasping their own bodies. As the monkeys grew older, this contact or subversion of contact with other individuals expressed itself in their not grooming other individuals and in real problems in efforts to reproduce. Even though sexual arousal was evident, these monkeys did not know how to copulate properly. Furthermore, among those females who became pregnant in spite of their sexual deficiencies, the preponderance of mothers did not take care of their offspring. These and other demonstrations of the long-term consequences of contact deprivation were profound (H. F. Harlow & M. K. Harlow, 1971).

Twenty years ago, H. F. Harlow and I devised a therapeutic intervention for monkeys reared in isolation (Suomi & H. F. Harlow,

1972). The intervention was built on the fact that normal young monkeys have a tendency to cling to their partners. We introduced 3-month-old monkey "therapists," who were still at the clinging stage, to these older isolates. The younger monkeys initiated contact with these isolates, and very quickly, the isolates turned around and began to reciprocate the contact. When one is contacting another monkey, it is difficult to engage in much self-directed behavior. Eventually these isolate monkeys began actively interacting with the therapists and subsequently showed relatively normal social and emotional development. The therapeutic power of touch was quite evident in these early rehabilitation studies on isolated monkeys, and these data stand to this day.

Contact had another possible therapeutic consequence in these isolated monkeys. Early studies indicated that most females who were reared in isolation and became mothers themselves had problems taking care of their offspring, but Harlow's group, and later some of our own work, indicated that if these females had short periods of contact with an infant, whether they took adequate care of that infant or not, they became perfectly normal mothers with subsequent offspring. That is, a little bit of contact (at least 48 hours) with a first-born offspring, even though it may not have been entirely positive, seemed to prime them so that virtually every one turned out to be a perfectly normal mother toward subsequent offspring (Ruppenthal, Arling, H. F. Harlow, Sackett, & Suomi, 1976; Suomi & Ripp, 1983). Once again, we see the therapeutic power of touch.

What does this have to do with immunology? The diagram in Fig. 8.9, by Mark Laudenslager, one of the primatologists doing pioneering immunological work, illustrates the complexity of the immune system and the variety of organs that are involved in immunological responses; each of the various components is involved in a different immunological response. It also shows that the immune system is connected to a variety of organs involved in stress reactions—the hypothalamus, the pituitary, and the adrenal—and a great deal of sympathetic innervation. The functioning of the immunological system is reflected in the body's response to challenge (possibly as a by-product of interactions with the organs involved in stress hormone production), and consequences of various early experiences are expressed in the immunological system.

Coe, Lubach, Ershler, and Klopp (1989) have demonstrated a variety of deficits in the immunological systems in monkeys who are raised away from their mothers during the first few months of

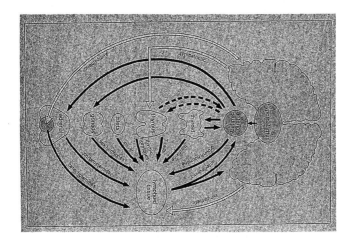

FIG. 8.9. Schematic diagram of interaction pathways between immune system and other biological systems in primate (from Laudenslager, 1991).

life compared to those who have early maternal experience. Although mother-reared and non–mother-reared monkeys show relatively similar patterns of behavior, they still exhibit significant differences in the responsiveness of their immunological systems to mitogen challenge. In particular, non–mother-reared monkeys display unusually high levels of lymphocyte proliferation following exposure to pokeweed and Concanabin A, and these differential responses are still apparent in middle and late childhood.

We have been interested, more recently, in assessing differential stress responses in monkeys with different rearing conditions, particularly because of the connections between the immunological system and the organs producing the adrenal hormones and the catecholamines.

Figure 8.10 shows "together–together" reared monkeys. These are monkeys reared in the absence of a mother, but with extensive peer experience. They have many opportunities for contact, perhaps too many: Instead of playing with each other as normal peers do, they develop mutual clinging patterns. For a variety of reasons, they seem to be more susceptible, both behaviorally and physiologically, to both simple and more complicated stressors.

During adolescence, when these animals are frightened they seek infant-like contact with one another, something no self-respecting

FIG. 8.10. Mutual clinging in your peer-reared (together–together)
rhesus monkeys.

mother-reared adolescent would do at this age (Fig. 8.11). These
peer-reared monkeys also exhibited an elevated stress hormone
response, in addition to increased monoamine turnover. In particular, monkeys reared by their mothers show less self-directed hud-
dling behavior following separation than monkeys reared in peer
groups. Peer-reared monkeys show higher plasma cortisol levels to
brief separation than mother-reared monkeys. In addition, peer-
reared monkeys, in both the first and the second years of life, reacted
to brief separations with much higher levels of ACTH and MHPG
(the metabolite of norepinephrine) than did their mother-reared
counterparts (Higley, Suomi, & Linnoila, 1992).

Currently, we are trying to determine whether different rearing
conditions and responses to stress give rise to differential immunological responses. Given the interactive nature of the relationship
between the immune system and other systems, it is difficult to
imagine that we would not see variability associated with differences
in the early experiences of these monkeys. There is something magi-
cal about the intense social stimulation that monkeys receive in
normal social groups. We are now focusing on the extent to which
we can reproduce the stimulation that newborn rhesus monkeys
normally receive when they are growing up in the wild.

We have also looked at the response of antibodies to stress, the
basis of most vaccinations. The typical immunological response to a

FIG. 8.11. Mutual clinging in adolescent peer-reared monkeys.

primary anthragen challenge, which in this case can be a vaccination (e.g., a tetanus shot) is an increase in the immunoglobulins IgM and IgG. These initially rise in response to the challenge and then return to baseline. If one receives the equivalent of a booster shot, a secondary response is elicited, which is even bigger than the first. This is the rationale underlying the series of shots that newborn human infants get, which are then followed by booster shots.

The question we are asking is whether, in a naturalistic setting, there is any relationship between touch and the reaction to stress and the body's ability to manufacture the appropriate response to an immunological challenge. These studies were carried out on an island in Puerto Rico run by the Caribbean Primate Research Center, where some of us from the NIH have been graciously allowed to work. A natural population of rhesus monkeys has been living on the island, more or less unrestrained, for the last 52 years. There are now 1,400 monkeys on the island (Fig. 8.12). Once a year, the monkeys are rounded up for their annual medical checkup. They

FIG. 8.12. Rhesus monkeys on Cayo Santiago Island.

are given a tetanus shot, a tuberculosis test, and are weighed and measured; the other 364 days of the year, they are left undisturbed.

One of our interests was determining whether infants in this situation would develop a healthy antibody response to a tetanus inoculation, and whether the magnitude of that response was related in any way to either their biobehavioral response to challenge or to their pattern of mother–infant contact. What we saw was that there was a direct relationship between the amount of contact and grooming an infant received during its first 6 or 7 months of life and its ability to produce antibody titer in response to an antibody challenge at a little over 1 year of age (Laudenslager, Rasmussen, Berman, Suomi, & Berger, 1993). So, early contact experience seems to be related to the body's ability to respond to a tetanus shot and produce an appropriate antibody response later on. This is clearly a health-related outcome.

We hope to continue to do studies like this on the island. We would like to look at other responses to stress, as they occur both in nature and in the laboratory. These findings continue to tell us how important contact comfort and touch are for rhesus monkeys. The lessons that we learn should be valid not only for the rhesus monkeys that we study, but for their human counterparts, so that insights from our work with primates can enhance our basic understanding of the effects of human touch.

Steve Suomi—Question and Answer Session

QUESTION: Would you comment on the fact that when you put a small baby in day-care, you can predict that they will have otitis media in the next 4 months. Is there anything we can do about that?

ANSWER: The inference I would make is that this is a stressor for the infant. The stressor may be compromising some aspects of the immune system. I don't know if it would help to have the mother come with the child initially to make that transition less extreme.

QUESTION: You mentioned that you were making an effort to artificially simulate the types of stimulation the mother gives to the baby. Can you comment on that?

ANSWER: Yes, we are using a variety of techniques. One of them is cross-fostering infants who differ in temperament. Because temperament seems to be highly heritable, it is possible to rear infants who have been selectively bred for particular types of temperament with foster mothers that provide differing degrees of contact and/or other aspects of maternal care, such as rejection patterns. We can also control the content of the social group in which the infant is growing up and the presence of older siblings and other adults. We have done some work limiting interactions with peers to certain types of peers at only particular periods of time. Many of the consequences of peer-rearing, such as the extreme levels of clinging and the extreme reactions to stress, seem to be minimized when, paradoxically, instead of letting these peers interact for 24 hours a day, they only interact for 2 hours a day. When that happens, their interactions during those 2 hours are much like what happens in a school recess: You have active playing, rather than clinging. In that sense, these animals seem to be more normal in terms of their response to subsequent challenge later in life. Finally, we have been using puppets, having them interact in particular patterns with these infants. We are particularly interested in tactile stimulation initiated by human caretakers to infants while they are in the neonatal nursery. While we do these manipulations, we monitor a variety of behaviors and physiological systems, including some of the immunological systems.

QUESTION: Does this have implications for autism?

ANSWER: I am not sure, in terms of physiological characteristics. Many years ago, a number of investigators pointed out the behavioral similarities between some aspects of autistic child behavior, particularly the self-directed and stereotypic activities, and the apparent shutting out of interest in social stimulation. With the behavior of monkeys reared in isolation, who, among other things, do develop such stereotypies, what is apparent is that, whereas you would get these effects in monkeys following isolation, most autistic children are not reared in that degree of social isolation unless it is functional social isolation. If there is something in the child's makeup that prevents him or her from interacting socially, either because of the stimulus coming in or because of his or her response system, the kinds of resultant behaviors would seem to be direct consequences of that lack of social interaction. So, to the extent that autistic children self-isolate, then some of the behavioral similarities that you see with the isolated monkeys would seem to make sense.

REFERENCES

Bowlby, J. (1969). *Attachment.* New York: Basic Books.

Coe, C. L., Lubach, G., Ershler, W. B., & Klopp, R. G. (1989). Influence of early rearing on lymphocyte proliferation response in juvenile monkeys. *Brain, Behavior, and Immunity, 3,* 47–60.

Fairbanks, L. A. (1989). Early experience and cross-generational continuity of mother–infant contact in vervet monkeys. *Developmental Psychobiology, 27,* 660–681.

Harlow, H. F. (1958). The nature of love. *American Psychologist, 13,* 673–685.

Harlow, H. F., & Harlow, M. K. (1962). Social deprivation in monkeys. *Scientific American, 207,* 136–144.

Harlow, H. F., & Harlow, M. K. (1971). Psychopathology in monkeys. In H. Kimmel (Ed.), *Experimental psychopathology* (pp. 203–229). New York: Academic Press.

Harlow, H. F., & Zimmerman, R. R. (1959). Affectional responses in the infant monkey. *Science, 130*, 421–432.

Higley, J. D., Suomi, S. J., & Linnoila, M. (1992). A longitudinal assessment of CSF monoamine metabolite and plasma cortisol concentrations in young rhesus monkeys. *Biological Psychiatry, 32*, 127–145.

Laudenslager, M. L., Rasmussen, K. L., Berman, C. M., Suomi, S. J., & Berger, C. B. (1993). Specific antibody levels in free-ranging rhesus monkeys: Relationships to plasma hormones, cardiac parameters, and early behavior. *Developmental Psychobiology, 26*, 407–420.

Ruppenthal, G. C., Arling, G. L., Harlow, H. F., Sackett, G. P., & Suomi, S. J. (1976). A 10-year perspective on motherless mother monkey behavior. *Journal of Abnormal Psychology, 85*, 341–349.

Suomi, S. J., Champoux, M., & Higley, J. D. (1994). *Cross-generational transmission of specific maternal behavior patterns in rhesus monkeys.* Unpublished manuscript.

Suomi, S. J., & Harlow, H. F. (1972). Social rehabilitation of isolate-reared monkeys. *Developmental Psychology, 6*, 487–496.

Suomi, S. J., & Ripp, C. (1983). A history of motherless mother monkey mothering at the University of Wisconsin Primate Laboratory. In M. Reite & N. Caine (Eds.), *Child abuse: The nonhuman primate data* (pp. 49–78). New York: Alan R. Liss.

CHAPTER NINE

Infant Massage Therapy

Tiffany Field
University of Miami School of Medicine

Infant massage is a common child-care practice in many parts of the world, especially in Africa and Asia: in Nigeria, Uganda, India, Bali, Fiji, New Guinea, New Zealand (the Maiori), Venezuela, and the Soviet Union (Auckett, 1981). In most of these countries, the infant is given a massage with oil following the daily bath and prior to sleep time, for the first several months of life.

INFANT MASSAGE IN THE WESTERN WORLD

Infant massage has only recently been discovered and researched in the Western world. In the United States, for example, massage therapy schools are beginning to teach infant massage. Infant massage therapists have founded a national organization of approximately 4,000 therapists, and those therapists are setting up institutes to teach parents infant massage. The techniques they use are based primarily on the teachings of two massage therapists who trained in India: Amelia Auckett, who published a book on infant massage in 1981, and Vimala Schneider McClure, who published a similar book on infant massage in 1989.

105

Although these infant massage training groups are located in most parts of the United States, very little research has been conducted on the use of infant massage with healthy infants. Nonetheless, the infant massage training groups have anecdotally reported that massage: (a) facilitates the parent–infant bonding process in the development of warm, positive relationships; (b) reduces stress responses to painful procedures, such as inoculations; (c) reduces the pain associated with teething and constipation; (d) reduces colic; (e) helps induce sleep; and (f) makes parents "feel good" while they are massaging their infants. Infant massage therapy groups have also reported that several different kinds of infants with special needs appear to benefit from infant massage. These include infants who are blind and deaf, who become more aware of their bodies; cerebral palsied; and preterm.

MASSAGE THERAPY WITH PRETERM INFANTS

Most of the data on the positive effects of infant massage come from studies on preemies. Since the 1970s, a number of investigators have researched the effects of massage therapy (earlier called *tactile/kinesthetic stimulation*) on the preterm newborn (Barnard & Bee, 1983; Rausch, 1981; Rice, 1975; Solkoff & Matuszak, 1975; White & LaBarba, 1976). Their results have generally been positive. In a recent meta-analysis on 19 of these stimulation studies,Ottenbacher et al. (1987) estimated that 72% of infants receiving some form of tactile stimulation were positively affected. Most investigators have reported greater weight gain and better performance on developmental tasks for the preterm infants receiving massage therapy. Interestingly, those who did not report significant weight gain used a light stroking procedure, which has since been found to be aversive to babies, probably because it is experienced as tickling. Those who showed weight gain experienced more pressure, which probably stimulated both tactile and pressure receptors.

One of the studies used in this meta-analysis was conducted in our lab starting in 1984. In that study, we gave 20 preterm neonates 45 minutes of massage per day (in doses of three 15-minute periods) for 10 days (Field et al., 1986). The infants averaged 31 weeks gestational age, 1,280 grams birth weight, and 20 days of intensive care prior to the time of the study. They were recruited for the study when they had graduated from the "grower nursery," at a time when their primary agenda was to gain weight. The massage sessions consisted of three 5-minute phases. During the first and third phases, tactile stimulation was given. The newborn was placed in a prone position and given moderate pressure stroking of the head and face region, neck and shoulders, back, legs, and arms for 1 minute each. The Swedish-like massage was given because, as already noted, infants prefer some degree of pressure. The middle (kinesthetic) phase involved flexing of the infants' limbs (moving them into flexion and then extension much like bicycling motions) while the infant was lying on his or her back.

This study yielded a number of interesting findings:

1. The massaged infants in this study gained 47% more weight than the unmassaged controls, even though the groups did not differ in calorie intake (see Fig. 9.1).
2. The massaged infants were awake and active a greater percentage of the observation time than the controls, much to our surprise; we had expected that massage would stimulate a soporific state and greater sleep time, which would lead to weight gain because of a decrease in energy expenditure.
3. The massaged infants showed better performance on the Brazelton Scale on habituation, orientation, motor activity, and regulation of state behavior.
4. The massaged infants averaged 6 days less in the hospital than the control infants, yielding a cost saving of approximately $3,000 per infant.

Simultaneously, our collaborator, Saul Schanberg, was conducting studies with Cynthia Kuhn at Duke University on an animal model, removing rat pups from their mothers to investigate touch deprivation and attempting to simulate the mothers' behavior to restore the physiology and biochemistry of these rat pups to normal. In several studies, they noted the fall in ornithine decarboxylase (ODC), a critical element in the protein synthesis chain (Schanberg & Field, 1988). This decrease in ODC was noted in all body organs, including the heart and liver, and in parts of the brain, including the cerebrum, cerebellum, and brain stem; these values returned to normal once the pups were stimulated. A graduate student observing the rat mothers' nocturnal behavior noted that they frequently

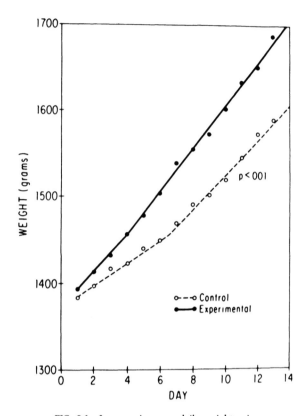

FIG. 9.1. Increase in mean daily weight gain.

tongue lick, pinch, and carry around the rat pups. Each of these maneuvers was tried, but only the tongue licking (simulated by a paint brush dipped in water and briskly stroked all over the body of the rat pup) restored these values to their normal levels. More recently, Schanberg and his colleagues discovered a growth gene that responds to tactile stimulation (an early immediate gene, labeled C-FOS), suggesting genetic origins of this touch–growth relationship.

Realizing that an exploration of under-the-skin variables including physiology and biochemistry, might suggest an underlying mechanism in the human model, we added physiological and biochemical measures to our next study. This study, again with preterm infants, basically confirmed our previous findings. In this sample, the stimulated infants showed a 21% greater daily weight gain, were discharged 5 days earlier, showed superior performance on the

Brazelton Habituation items, and exhibited fewer stress behaviors (mouthing, grimacing, and clenching fists) than the control infants (Scafidi et al., 1990). In addition, we noted that their catecholamines (norepinephrine, epinephrine) had increased across the stimulation period (Kuhn et al., 1991). Although these catecholamines typically increase following stress in the adult, suggesting that an increase is undesirable, an increase during the neonatal period is considered desirable, because there is a normal developmental increase following birth. Thus, massage therapy apparently facilitates the normal developmental increase in these catecholamines in stimulated preterm infants. In the interim, we also discovered that their vagal activity increased during massage therapy sessions.

These observations, plus the work of Uvnas-Moberg in Sweden, led us to some ideas about underlying mechanisms. Uvnas-Moberg and her colleagues have reported that stimulating the inside of the mouth of the newborn led to the increased release of gastrointestinal food absorption hormones in the infant, such as gastrin and insulin (Uvnas-Moberg, Widstrom, Marchine, & Windberg, 1987). It is conceivable that another form of tactile stimulation, such as the massage therapy on different body parts, could also lead to the release of gastrointestinal food absorption hormones, probably stimulated by vagal activity. Thus, we are currently assaying glucose and insulin levels in the heel-stick blood samples of preterm infants. Our preliminary data suggest that the massaged infants have elevated levels of both glucose and insulin.

MASSAGING COCAINE-EXPOSED PRETERM INFANTS

In the interim, a relative newcomer to the neonatal intensive care unit (NICU), the cocaine-exposed preterm infant, has provided us with another sample of infants that might be helped by massage therapy. In this study, the same type of massage was administered three times daily for a 10-day period, with the hope that much the same effects would occur. Compared to nonmassaged infants, the massaged cocaine-exposed preterm infants: (a) had fewer postnatal complications and exhibited fewer stress behaviors during the 10 day period, (b) had a 28% greater daily weight gain, and (c) demonstrated more mature motor behavior on the Brazelton exam at the end of the 10-day period (Wheeden, Scafidi, Field, Ironson, & Valdeon, in press).

MASSAGING HIV-EXPOSED NEONATES

Still a more recent newcomer to the NICU are HIV-exposed infants. Dr. Scafidi and our colleagues are currently investigating whether massage therapy also improves immune functioning in HIV-exposed newborns and whether massage therapy given by parents can improve the mental, motor, and social development of the infants, as well as giving the mothers a greater sense of worth and decreasing their guilt feelings for having transmitted this disease to their infants. We have noted very impressive compliance on the part of the HIV mothers: Almost 100% compliance in their administering three massages per day to their infants for the first 2 weeks of life. Compared to nonmassaged infants, the massaged infants exhibit: (a) greater weight gain; (b) better performance on the orientation and motor clusters of the Brazelton scale; and (c) better performance on a stress behavior scale, including alert responsiveness, examiner persistence, state regulation, motor tone, and excitability.

DEPRESSED MOTHERS MASSAGING
THEIR INFANTS

We need a cost-effective way to deliver massage therapy to infants. Furthermore, parents as massage therapists may benefit from *giving* the massage, and the parent–infant relationship may improve. Therefore, we are increasingly teaching parents to administer massage therapy in our studies. In a current study, we are teaching depressed mothers to massage their infants to examine the effects of the massage therapy on the infants' disorganized interaction behavior and their disturbed sleep patterns (see Fig. 9.2). For this study, we have asked each infant's primary caregiver to perform a 15-minute massage daily for a 2-week period. Preliminary results suggest the following:

1. Drowsiness and quiet sleep increased immediately following the massage, and activity decreased, as would be expected.

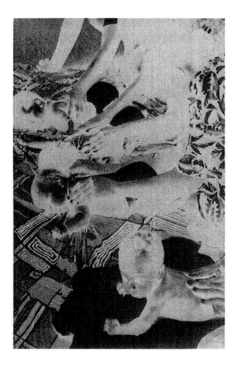

FIG. 9.2. Depressed adolescent mothers massaging their infants.

2. The infants' latency to sleep was shorter following the massage therapy study: By the end of the 2-week period, the latency to sleep decreased from 22 minutes to 9 minutes.

3. The infants showed increased vocalizations, decreased restlessness, and improved affect during mother–infant play interactions, and the mothers' play behavior became more age appropriate.

4. The infants' fussiness decreased after the 2-week period.

5. The infants' depressed mothers perceived their "depressed" infants as being easier to soothe.

These data on decreased fussiness and more organized sleep suggested that we should conduct studies having parents massage their colicky infants and their infants with sleep disturbances. Thus, we are using the same model for those groups.

GRANDPARENT VOLUNTEERS
AS MASSAGE THERAPISTS

Another cost-effective way to deliver massage therapy is via "grand-parent" volunteers. In an ongoing study, grandparent volunteers are being trained to massage neglected and abused children in a shelter. The study is designed to measure the effects of massage therapy on sexually and physically abused children living in a nearby shelter, as well as the effects on the volunteer grandparents of their giving the massage. (It is interesting that the other end of the age spectrum, the elderly, also experiences failure to thrive, probably as a second-ary outcome of touch deprivation.)

A recent survey indicated that failure-to-thrive was the admitting diagnosis in 57% of elderly admitted to acute care teaching hospitals (Campion, Berkman, & Fulmer, 1986). Clinical depression, on the other hand, is the most common psychiatric disorder among the elderly, with prevalence rates estimated between 5% and 26% (Copeland et al., 1987; Gaylord & Zung, 1987). Depressive symp-tomatology in the elderly is similar to that in younger persons, including anhedonia, poor concentration, and feelings of hopeless-ness and worthlessness. On the other hand, complaints of ill-defined physical problems and memory impairments may be present in other elderly people in the absence of complaints of depressed mood or dysphoria (Post, 1982). As is true of depression at other ages, one might expect effects on physiology, including frequent night wakings, increased urinary cortisol levels, and decreased levels of immunocompetence. These depression effects may contribute to the failure-to-thrive syndrome in the elderly, as they do in infants who are depressed and failing to thrive. Pet therapy data suggest that volunteer grandparents may gain as much from giving a massage as from getting a massage (Grossberg & Alf, 1985).

In our study on volunteer grandparents who received massage and were also trained to give massages to neglected and abused infants, the preliminary results for the infants include: (a) drowsiness and quiet sleep increased and activity decreased following massage; (b) after 1 month of massage therapy, alertness and tracking behaviors increased; and (c) behavioral observations suggested increased activ-ity, sociability, and soothability. As for the volunteer grandparents, (a) they reported less anxiety and fewer depression symptoms and an improved mood after receiving massages; (b) their cortisol levels decreased; (c) their lifestyles improved, with more social contacts, fewer trips to doctors' offices, and fewer cups of coffee; and (d) they reported improved self-esteem. These effects on the grandparents appeared to be even greater following the month of giving versus the month of receiving their own massages. These data suggest the power of massage therapy not only for infants, but for the adults who massage them, making volunteer infant massage more than just cost effective.

REFERENCES

Auckett, A. D. (1981). *Baby massage*. New York: Newmarket Press.

Barnard, K. E., & Bee, H. L. (1983). The impact of temporally patterned stimulation on the development of preterm infants. *Child Development, 54*, 1156–1167.

Campion, E., Berkman, B., & Fulmer, T. (1986). *Failure to thrive in the elderly* [hospital survey, unpublished report]. Cambridge, MA: Harvard University Medical School.

Copeland, J. R. M., Dewey, M. E., Wood, N., Searle, R., Davidson, I. A., & McWilliams, C. (1987). Range of mental illness among the elderly in the community: Prevalence in Liverpool using the GMS-AGECAT package. *British Journal of Psychiatry, 150*, 815–823.

Field, T., Schanberg, S., Scafidi, F., Bower, C., Vega-Lahr, N., Garcia, R., Nystrom, J., & Kuhn, C. M. (1986). Tactile/kinesthetic stimulation effects on preterm neonates. *Pediatrics, 77*, 654–658.

Gaylord, S. A., & Zung, W. W. K. (1987). Affective disorders among the aging. In L. L. Carstensen & B. A. Edelstein (Eds.), *Handbook of clinical gerontology* (pp. 19–35). New York: Pergamon.

Grossberg, J. M., & Alf, E. F., Jr. (1985). Interaction with pet dogs: Effects on human cardiovascular response. *Journal of the Delta Society, 8*, 20–27.

Kuhn, C., Schanberg, S., Field, T., Symanski, R., Zimmerman, E., Scafidi, F., & Roberts, J. (1991). Tactile-kinesthetic stimulation effects on sympathetic and adrenocortical function in preterm infants. *Journal of Pediatrics, 119*, 434–440.

McClure, V. S. (1989). *Infant massage*. New York: Bantam.

Ottenbacher, K. J., Muller, L., Brandt, D., Heintzelman, A., Hojem, P., & Sharpe, P. (1987). The effectiveness of tactile stimulation as a form of early intervention: A quantitative evaluation. *Journal of Developmental and Behavioral Pediatrics, 8*, 68–76.

Post, F. (1982). Functional disorders: II. Treatment and its relationship to causation. In R. Levy & F. Post (Eds.), *The psychiatry of late life* (pp. 39–46). London: Blackwell.

Rausch, P. B. (1981). Effects of tactile and kinesthetic stimulation on premature infants. *Journal of Obstetric, Gynecological and Neonatal Nursing, 10*, 34–37.

Rice, R. D. (1977). Neurophysiological development in premature infants following stimulation. *Developmental Psychology, 13*, 69–76.

Scafidi, F., Field, T., Schanberg, S., Bauer, C., Tucci, K., Roberts, J., Morrow, C., & Kuhn, C.M. (1990). Massage stimulates growth in preterm infants: A replication. *Infant Behavior and Development, 13,* 167–188.

Schanberg, S., & Field, T. (1988). Maternal deprivation and supplemental stimulation. In T. Field, P. McCabe, & N. Schneiderman (Eds.), *Stress and coping across development* (pp. 116–143). Hillsdale, NJ: Lawrence Erlbaum Associates.

Solkoff, N., & Matuszak, D. (1975). Tactile stimulation and behavioral development among low-birthweight infants. *Child Psychiatry and Human Development, 6,* 33–37.

Uvnas-Moberg, K., Widstrom, A. M., Marchine, G., & Windberg, J. (1987). Release of GI hormone in mothers and infants by sensory stimulation. *Acta Paediatrica Scandinavia, 76,* 851–860.

Wheeden, A., Scafidi, F. A., Field, T., Ironson, G., & Valdeon, C. (1993). Massage effects on cocaine-exposed preterm neonates. *Developmental and Behavioral Pediatrics, 14,* 318–322.

White, J. L., & LaBarba, R. C. (1976). The effects of tactile and kinesthetic stimulation on neonatal development in the premature infant. *Developmental Psychobiology, 6,* 569–577.

Author Index

Subject Index